Elnora

THE GIRL WITH THE VIOLIN

BY HEATHER SHUMAKER

MARGARET THATCHER WROTE: "BEING POWERFUL IS A LOT LIKE BEING A LADY, IF YOU HAVE TO TELL PEOPLE YOU ARE, YOU PROBABLY AREN'T." FROM THE MOMENT I BEGAN TO PAINT ELNORA'S PORTRAIT, I KNEW I WAS IN THE PRESENCE OF A LADY ... NOBODY HAD TO TELL ME SO. —W. TRUMAN HOSNER

Copyright © 2015 by Elnora Milliken
All rights reserved.
Cover art by William Truman Hosner, 2013
Published by Mission Point Press
www.missionpointpress.com

Contents

PART I

MINNESOTA DAYS
SONGS OF ITALY
MINNESOTA MUSIC
THE IRON RANGE

PART II

COLLEGE AND MUSIC TEACHING
CHICAGO
DETROIT

PART III

MARRIED LIFE
DR. JOHN
EARLY MARRIED LIFE

PART IV

HOME IN TRAVERSE CITY
MILLIKEN MEDICAL BEGINS
PENINSULA DRIVE
CHILDREN AND MUSIC
WENDY'S SONG

PART V

ARTS PIONEER
A TRAVERSE SYMPHONY
OLD TOWN PLAYHOUSE

PART VI

MUSIC, GARDENS AND ADVENTURES
THE FRIENDLY GARDEN CLUB
MUSIC AND INTERLOCHEN PUBLIC RADIO
MILLIKEN MEDICAL ORCHESTRA
BOATING AND RV TRIPS

PART VII

ADVANCING
GROWING FAMILY
ALWAYS ADVANCING
MORE FAMILY PHOTOS

ELNORA'S HIGH
SCHOOL PHOTO

PART I

Minnesota Days

SONGS OF ITALY

Dammi baci del amor

Dammi, dammi, dammi baci del amor

A la spinola se mi baci così

Baci, baci da noche di…

Elnora's story begins with music. She was born into a house of joyful singing where music and musical instruments were part of each day. Some of the first melodies she heard were Italian love songs her father and mother used to sing around the house, such as Dammi baci del amor (give me a kiss). Soon she became known as "the girl with the violin" and went on to spread a lifetime of joyful music to friends, family, students and communities in many places, especially Minnesota and Michigan.

Elnora was born on Thanksgiving Day, November 25, in a year that seems like yesterday in Chisholm, Minnesota. Chisholm was part of the famous Iron Range, and it was bursting with international vibrancy as immigrants flocked to northern Minnesota to work in the Mesabi iron ore mines. Like many Chisholm families, Elnora's parents had emigrated from Italy, from a region near Milan and Turino in the northwest, known as Piemonte, also known as Piedmont. They both spoke piemontèis, a language that mixed elements of Italian and French.

She was christened Eleonora Duce Toldo, (pronounced doo-chay) a name which means shining light. Her parents named her after a great Italian actress, not knowing she would live up to her name with her love of the stage. Elnora had one older sister, Muffi, or Mafalda, named after a big, beautiful ship. Muffi was two years older.

Elnora's father, Pietro Toldano, went by Peter Toldo in Chisholm. He arrived in New York City through Ellis Island in 1918. Like many new immigrants, he saw ads for good-paying work in Minnesota and headed west. He settled in Chisholm for work in the iron ore mines. The Chisholm mines opened in 1900 after the Mesabi iron ore was discovered. Like other boomtowns across the Iron Range, Chisholm grew rapidly. During its prime years in the 1920s, Chisholm had a population of 10,000, mostly Italian, Finnish, Czech, Polish plus other Slavic people.

Elnora's mother, Lucia Savio, was one of seven children. She grew up in the beautiful mountain town of Cuorgnè, near Turino, where her family owned a large orchard that grew apples, peaches and grapes. Her father loved America and had visited more than once. His dream was to sell his house and acreage in Italy and settle in America. But in the end, he did not go, since his wife wanted to stay in Italy. Instead, he encouraged his children to move to the United States.

Lucia was only nineteen when she embarked for America. She cried, but left Italy because her father told her she would have a beautiful life in the U.S. When she hugged her father goodbye she said "I'll see you soon." But she never saw him again.

Her boat crossing took three weeks. When Lucia arrived at Ellis Island, she felt great relief to get off the boat. Buoyed by her father's words, she tried to be courageous, but she was also filled with longing for her family. She had left three sisters behind in Italy, as well as her parents. One sister, Manya, and two brothers were already in America. The two brothers settled in Indiana where one became a builder and the other one had a horse farm.

Lucia and Peter met at a dance band in nearby Virginia, Minnesota. Lucia was there dancing and Peter was playing violin, mandolin and guitar in the band. They discovered they were both living in Chisholm and began to see each other.

The first thing both Lucia and Peter each did when they arrived in Chisholm was to sign up for English classes. These classes were given at the local high school, and they both quickly learned English. Before she met Peter, Lucia took a job at a hotel. The hotel manager was so impressed by her voice that he offered to teach her English if she would read aloud to him. The hotel manager adored her. Later, when Lucia announced she was engaged to Peter, the manager presented her with a diamond ring as a wedding gift.

Lucia's hotel earnings came in handy. On their wedding day, Peter's convertible broke down. He didn't have enough money to fix it, so Lucia reached into her savings from the hotel and paid to have the car fixed.

OPEN PIT MINING IN CHISOLM, MN

Both Elnora's parents were young when they got married and started a family. They were full of endless energy and optimism for their new life.

Peter worked in open-pit mines and in other jobs for the mining company, but he would not work underground. Miners who descended into the pits to dig iron ore got higher pay, but Peter preferred being safe on the ground in the daylight. Besides mining, Peter and Lucia tended extensive gardens, and grew vegetables, berries and flowers for their own family and to sell. They sold flowers to hotels in Hibbing and Virginia. They also sold their garden's bounty, including cases of raspberries and strawberries, at the farmer's market in Hibbing.

Elnora was ahead of her time.. She even walked at a very early age. One day when she was only six and a half months old, her mother left her in the baby buggy near the house while she worked busily in the garden. The next-door neighbor saw Elnora kicking her feet and crying. She cried so hard that the neighbor, Mrs. Simonson, said to Elnora's mother: "Bring the buggy over here and I'll take care of her while you garden." Lucia brought Elnora over to Mrs. Simonson, but Elnora kept crying and kicking, so Mrs. Simonson put Elnora down on the ground. She was so startled when Elnora started walking. She quickly put Elnora back in the buggy. "Lucia, Lucia! She's walking! She's walking!" she cried from next door.

MINNESOTA MUSIC

Peter, Elnora's father, was a natural musician. He played the mandolin, guitar and violin. Peter never had a lesson in his life, thanks to his absolute pitch, excellent rhythm and a deep love of music. Although mining was his livelihood, music was his life. He often said he was 'born too soon, ahead of his time.' While Elnora was growing up, he played in a jazz band and also marched and played trumpet with the Chisholm Drum and Bugle Corps. The Corps traveled by bus to play as far away as Florida, California and Canada, which was unusual at the time. One time Peter brought back beautiful sweaters for Muffi and Elnora from Canada.

Elnora loved music, too, and at first she tried the guitar. Her father said, "No, you're no good at that." Next she tried mandolin, thinking that was a nice instrument, but again he said: "No, no, you're not good." When she tried the violin he was pleased. "He said I was excellent so I played the violin." Elnora soon loved it in her own right. "The violin is so beautiful. You can express yourself. You can do anything in music with the violin."

CHISOLM DRUM AND BUGLE CHAMPIONS, 1942

Elnora was lucky to inherit her father's absolute pitch. This rare gift meant she could identify and reproduce exact musical notes without a reference pitch. She could name each note being played just by hearing it. She could also play a piece of music she had just heard, and tell whether music was being played sharp or flat. This was mostly a benefit, but sometimes caused her to wince, or even to leave a concert, if the music was being played too sharp or too flat.

She started violin lessons in second grade. By fourth grade, Elnora was taking violin lessons at the Lombardy Conservatory in Hibbing, had memorized Debussy's "Claire de Lune," on piano, and was playing in the Hibbing Symphony Orchestra. This was a full orchestra of sixty to seventy musicians, which drew musicians from Duluth to Grand Rapids, Minnesota as well as many smaller mining towns. Elnora was the only young child who played with the symphony orchestra. She sat last chair in the second violin section, but was thrilled to be playing with the symphony. Orchestra members made one dollar for attending rehearsals on Sunday afternoons. "That was like gold!" said Elnora. She saved her earnings in a little box.

The Hibbing Symphony was under the care of Luigi Lombardy and his wife, Ada, who was a pianist. They ran the Lombardy Conservatory in Hibbing, which was seven miles away from Chisholm. Since they were fellow Italians and lived only seven miles away, the Lombardys were family friends and took special care of Elnora. The Lombardys helped Elnora's parents find a good violin for her and a nice bow, knowing how vital a good instrument and a good bow would be. During symphony rehearsals, Luigi conducted while Ada listened for tone and musical feeling. She would call out "Luigi, no!" and he would reply, "Ada, yes!" Then they looked at each other, quietly spoke Italian, and the symphony resumed rehearsal.

Luigi Lombardy had wild, white hair. He would walk down the street playing the piccolo with his white hair flowing behind him. He knew every instrument and memorized the score so he never used music or had a music stand when he conducted. "He just lived his music," said Elnora. "That really impressed me. I've never played in another symphony where the conductor didn't use music to conduct." Young Elnora quickly learned the rules of playing in a professional-quality orchestra: never talk during rehearsal; if a string breaks, keep bowing. Once in the middle of Tchaikovsky's Fifth Symphony, Luigi's hair was flying and he called out

"More, more, more!" Just then Elnora's bridge fell down, but she kept bowing, just as she'd been told to do.

Elnora loved playing in the symphony. The Lombardys conveyed the history behind each piece so she could feel the music's emotions. She felt important being part of a grown-up symphony and quickly became known in Chisholm as "The Girl with the Violin." Besides rehearsals and concerts in Hibbing, the orchestra traveled to give concerts throughout the Iron Range which gave Elnora new experiences. On a concert trip to Duluth, Elnora was surprised to encounter such steep hills, and was terrified that the bus would careen down Duluth's steep inclines and land in Lake Superior.

Also in fourth grade, Elnora started piano lessons. These were home lessons. The piano teacher would come to the house once a week to teach both Elnora and Muffi. A one-hour lesson cost one dollar. Elnora often practiced piano and violin four hours a day as a child. "I loved to practice. I liked to get everything perfect," she said. "I always looked ahead to what I would play on Sunday."

Sunday afternoons were devoted to music. Her parents invited company over and Muffi and Elnora would perform for the guests. Her father would play his mandolin and guitar, sometimes playing Lara's theme from Dr. Zhivago on the mandolin, Elnora and her sister played piano or violin, or sometimes both, and Muffi, who had a beautiful singing voice, would sing. Their mother would sing, too, and sometimes Muffi and her mother would sing duets. After the performance, her mother or dad would pass the basket to guests in the room to collect money. If there happened to be no guests that day, her parents would still hold Sunday concerts and pass the basket, putting money in themselves. The money was used to buy music and pay for music lessons.

About the time Elnora was invited to join the Iron Range symphony, she began to play solos around Iron Range towns. Starting in fifth grade she played the organ for weddings. The organ was the pump kind, and Elnora had to push her leg muscles hard to get the tone out.

Besides formal lessons and performances, the Toldo family surrounded themselves with music. Every night the family would sing Italian and French songs and listen to music on the radio. There was another kind of music nearby, too: hillbilly music. Hillbillies camped in the hills near the edge of Chisholm, and Elnora could hear their drifting monotones over the fields and hills.

AT HOME IN TRAVERSE CITY, 1980'S

THE IRON RANGE

The Great Depression hit when Elnora was in grade school. "I remember it so well," she said. "The mines closed down. Father and all the miners were out of work." Elnora's mother got a housecleaning job to help make ends meet. She cleaned one house, the home of a prosperous family who owned a cigar factory. As a fourth grader, Elnora said to her mother: "Mama, when I grow up I'll get you lots and lots of cleaning business."

With the gardens, the family never went hungry. "We always had plenty to eat," said Elnora. "And we always had music. Music makes you happy."

Besides the vegetable garden and raspberry and strawberry beds, the family kept five chickens that laid brown eggs. At times, her mother would kill one of the chickens by twisting its neck. Then she cooked the chicken in the pressure cooker so they would have meat in the winter. Her mother made wonderful Italian dishes such as panatoni, ravioli, antipasto and Italian desserts, including homemade doughnuts and cookies. She baked homemade white bread and taught her daughters how to make ravioli from scratch.

They never wasted anything. Instead of throwing away soapsuds from washing the dishes, Elnora and Muffi would gather the extra soap and put it in the garden to control bugs. It was healthier that way, too, since they didn't use pesticides. If her mother used egg whites to make an angel food cake than she would also make a gold cake to use the egg yolks.

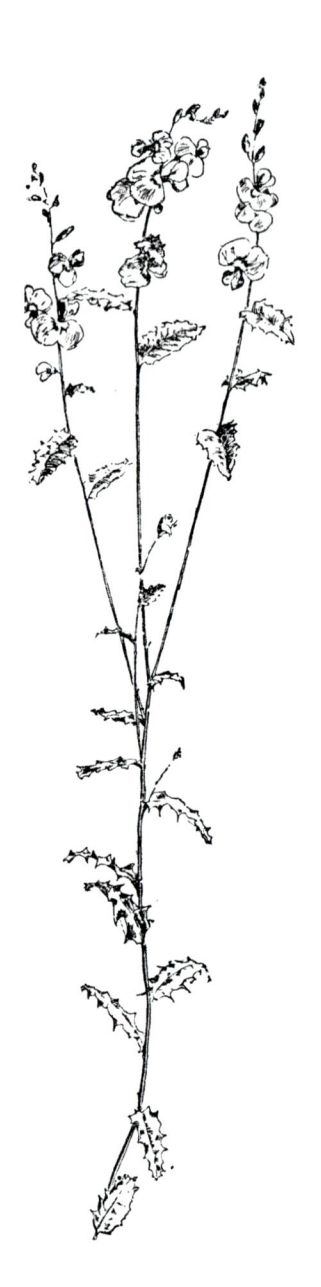

"Everyone on the Iron Range made wine," said Elnora. Her parents made white and red wine in the basement. Like everyone on the Range who made wine, her parents imported cases of grapes from California in September. Elnora's father would stomp on the grapes while her mother stood by and tasted it, saying "oh, there's too much sugar" or "not enough." They stored the wine in great barrels. Her mother would always bake homemade bread to go with the first wine of the season. "It was so delicious," said Elnora. The children loved dipping the fresh bread in the newly made wine each fall.

Lucia and Peter went mushroom hunting, too, bringing home mushrooms for their fresh antipasto, some of which they'd sell to people in Hibbing. To test and see if a mushroom was poisonous, they'd boil a nickel with it. If the nickel changed color, that meant the mushrooms were poisonous. The possibility of poisonous mushrooms made Elnora nervous, so she only nibbled them.

Besides music, the family always had flowers. "My father would go in the woods and get pussywillows and wildflowers." They also picked roses, gladiolas and peonies from their garden. Her mother would arrange the flowers and place them in a blue glass vase with a scalloped top, often peonies in pink, red and deep pink colors.

Her parents were always out working in the garden, and they typically wore overalls for garden work. When Elnora was in high school and had a special date, she used to say, "Mother and Dad, you can't meet so-and-so in your overalls! Get your overalls off, please! Can't you put something else on?" Then her parents would reply: "When you work in the garden you can't be dressed in fancy clothes. You have to wear clothes that can get dirty."

Muffi and Elnora worked in the garden, too. During the growing season, they would get up at four o'clock in the morning and tie a little pail around their waists. They put good raspberries in a quart basket and put spoiled raspberries in the little pail. Around eight o'clock that morning, they would pack everything up in the family's Plymouth to drive to the farmer's market in Hibbing. Muffi didn't like going, but Elnora loved helping at the farmer's market and the excitement of the crowds. Everyone knew them there. They were especially known for their raspberries, strawberries, vegetables and flowers, and people loved their high quality.

By this time the family had expanded to owning a second field in Chisholm, located two blocks down from their main garden by the house. This garden was mostly used for potatoes. Her mother canned a wide variety of the vegetables they grew in a great big pressure cooker. "My mother loved to can. She would can for the whole winter." They stored the canned food in the basement of their house, and also had a root cellar in the basement that they stocked with cabbages, squash, carrots and potatoes.

Her father was a believer in strength and exercise. He instructed his children to exercise or be active before sitting down to eat breakfast. He never had second helpings at meals and always drank a quarter glass of white wine with breakfast. Sometimes Elnora balked at all the healthy eating. One time as an adult, she developed a liking for ketchup. "For two years, my parents gave me a whole case of it for Christmas." After that, she didn't like ketchup at all.

The kitchen stove was the family's gathering place for breakfast. Half of the stove was electric, and the other half was wood-fired, like a fireplace. Elnora's parents put logs in the stove on cold mornings and the family would sit around enjoying the fire's warmth.

Winter in Chisholm, Minnesota brought extreme weather. Some years they got twelve feet of snow. When a big storm came through, the family could be snowbound, with snow so deep they couldn't get out the door for several days. When it finally stopped snowing, her father would shovel them out.

One time Elnora was walking home from school with her violin when a snowstorm hit. Her walk was about twelve blocks long. Already the wind was whipping up into a white-out and Elnora could barely stumble along. She thought: "Dear God, let me get home." Her father was waiting for her at the door and helped her crawl into the house. It was just in time. The family was snowbound for three days.

Once snug inside, snowbound days were joyful times. "We had so much fun. We sang and played music and mother cooked and made wonderful cookies and doughnuts."

WINTER IS STILL AN ENJOYABLE PART OF ELNORA'S LIFE (2009)

If a storm came up when Elnora was practicing music in Hibbing, she would be stranded there and have to spend the night at a friend's house. "They didn't have snow plows the way they do today," she said. "You couldn't get home if the Greyhound buses weren't running." Those who had cars made sure to stock up on food and blankets. It was quite possible to freeze to death on the roadside as nobody could come help.

Winter also was a wonderful time in the Iron Range. When the storms lifted, Elnora and her sister and friends would go sledding and skiing over the enormous banks of snow on their wooden skis. They also loved ice skating. Chisholm had many rinks, both indoor and outdoor. Every Saturday night her parents would go curling at the Civic Center downtown while the children ice skated next door. "All the parents would go. Mother and Father liked curling," she said.

When Muffi and Elnora walked to school in the winter, the only thing showing would be their eyes. All the children were bundled up, because otherwise their faces would freeze. In addition to their coats and regular clothes they wore woolen underwear. "We couldn't wait to stop wearing that wool underwear in spring!"

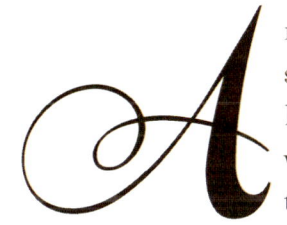

Another walk home from school was also traumatic. In eighth grade, Elnora was walking home from orchestra rehearsal in her new plaid jacket her mother had made. Suddenly a dog attacked her, ripping the back of her jacket. Elnora ran down the hill screaming. When she got home, her face was so white that her parents called a doctor. She was so scared she couldn't talk. Still to this day, she carries a deep fear of all dogs.

Elnora's interest in music grew as she entered high school. In addition to the Hibbing Symphony, she was invited to play in the Range symphony in Virginia, which she played in on and off. "I loved the symphony and thought I was in love with the first stand player," said Elnora. "He was in tenth grade and I was in eighth." Elnora played first violin in her high school orchestra, and at the end of ninth grade she stopped taking home piano lessons and began to study piano at the Lombardy Conservatory with Ada Lombardy. Elnora also took voice lessons for a short time, but like her father, her singing voice was not special. Muffi was the one who had the natural gift for beautiful singing, and she was a talented composer. Muffi wrote the senior class song for her high school graduation, and the school continued to use her song for several years.

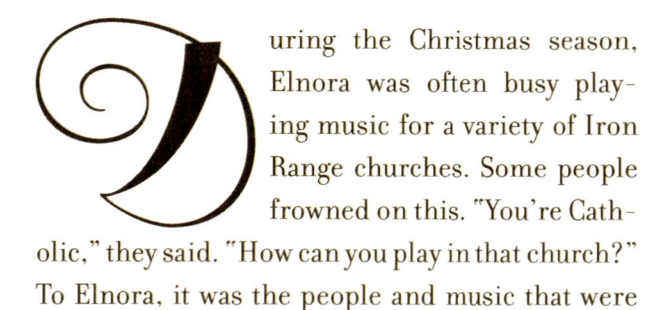

During the Christmas season, Elnora was often busy playing music for a variety of Iron Range churches. Some people frowned on this. "You're Catholic," they said. "How can you play in that church?" To Elnora, it was the people and music that were important.

Toward the end of Elnora's high school years, the Lombardys encouraged her parents to send Elnora to Italy to develop her musical ability. With her talent and absolute pitch, they were sure it was the right path. She had relatives living in Milan and Turino, Italy and they considered it a good opportunity for Elnora to perfect her musical skills. Her parents looked into sending her to Milan, home of La Scala Opera, but Elnora cried and fought the plan. "I couldn't go over there!" she said. "I didn't want to leave everything. I didn't want to leave home."

Another part of home that Elnora loved was Girl Scouting. She'd started early, as a Brownie, and by fifth grade she led her own troop of Brownie girls. Girl Scouting became an important part of her life as a teenager, and they frequently socialized with the Boy Scouts.

"Everyone was interested in Scouting on the Iron Range. You were so proud to be a Girl Scout or a Boy Scout. If you were a Scout you were respected and admired," she said. Scouting tended to attract the top students from all the nationalities who lived on the Iron Range. In honor of international Girl Scout Day, the girls would dress up in uniforms representing their heritage. Elnora represented Italy, and Chisholm scout troops had girls dressed in clothes from Slovenia, Finland, Bosnia, Poland and other countries. The scouts enjoyed helping people, and were sometimes involved in visiting houses where people were struggling with basic needs of food and shelter.

"I got every badge," said Elnora. "I sought every badge there was. I had an armful." One of the scout badges Elnora earned involved sleeping in a tree. "You had to make all the knots in a rope and sleep in a tree. You had a blanket but you slept in the tree alone. With just the moon out, it was an extraordinarily peaceful experience."

A highlight was going to Girl Scout camp at the Iron Range camp for one week each summer. The scouts worked hard pumping water and cleaning outdoor latrines. They loved it when the camp staff served dinner for breakfast and breakfast for dinner. "Every night we gathered by the campfire by the lake and sang Girl Scout songs under the stars," said Elnora.

During the winter they held sleigh ride parties and invited the Boy Scouts. On Saturday evenings Boy Scouts and Girl Scouts would meet up at a lake cottage owned by one of the families for ice fishing and dance parties. They'd play records on the Victrola phonograph by winding the hand crank and then dance.

Elnora loved to dance, especially swing dance. She taught dance steps to some of the high school boys, and they'd get together on some Sunday afternoons to practice swing moves and play live jazz songs. The high school held dances after school, and Elnora loved the thrill of the fast moves and partner dancing. She danced most with a boy named Leonard who was a very good dancer. They danced hot jazz together: fast dancing with lots of spins. "I loved it when he threw me over his shoulder. My parents sometimes watched the dances and were there when he threw me over his shoulder. They thought it was scandalous that I'd let him do that, but I loved it. It was so much fun!"

Like Chisholm itself, the high school was a mix of nationalities. Mr Vaughn, the school superintendent, urged all students to graduate from high school or college. Education was highly prized in the immigrant communities. The school itself was well funded with beautiful facilities, all made possible with iron mining royalties. The junior high and senior high each had two swimming pools, and the playgrounds and athletic fields were first-rate. In addition, the junior high and high school each had a spacious and comfortable auditorium for concerts and performances. The high school included a Dean of Girls who would take the whole class out for lunch once a year. On these special outings the girls wore hats and gloves and the Dean of Girls talked about good table manners.

In high school, Elnora discovered she loved to type. She used to arrive at school at 7am to practice typing on the school typewriters. "I wanted to go faster and faster. I'm the type who wants to do something the best ever possible." Elnora typed so fast the school invited her to enter a typing contest, but Elnora turned them down because she was too busy with her music.

When it came to prom time, Elnora was eager to find the best dancer to go with. She told some of the boys: "I may have to perform music that night, so I'm not sure I can go to prom with you." Then, when the right boy asked her, she'd accept happily. Most girls weren't invited to prom until they reached ninth grade, but Elnora attended as an eighth grader. "My mother made a beautiful pink dress for my eighth grade prom," said Elnora. Muffi hadn't been invited to prom that year, but soon she began to go steady in high school. Then it was Elnora's turn to be envious when Muffi received a large box of chocolates from her boyfriend on Valentine's Day, and Elnora, who dated many boys, only got cards. Elnora had one boyfriend who took her to the soda counter to get root beers, another boyfriend to go dancing with, and a third to go the movies. Chisholm showed new movies every week.

Acting became a new love in high school. Elnora decided she wanted to be an actress. After going to see movies in the theater, she would replay scenes in her head before falling asleep at night and imagine that she was in the movies. In school, she wanted to join the drama group, but there was some tension between the music and drama teachers. Mr. Regis, the high school music teacher, said she couldn't play first chair violin in the orchestra and be in theater. The drama teacher got around that. She announced that all graduating seniors had to audition for the senior play. When Elnora tried out, she got the lead. The news made headlines in the local paper, the Hibbing Daily Tribune.

It also made waves among some of the drama students, who'd been taking theater classes for years, and were disgruntled that a newcomer got the part. When some students refused to talk to her, Elnora sought advice from her parents. "My mother and father said, 'enjoy your part and do the best you can.'"

The play was The Youngest, by Philip Barry. As the leading lady, Elnora had to deal with having a dog on stage. She was still afraid of dogs, and her very first line was "Eustace, behave!" This chance to act on stage ignited a lifelong love of theater.

For high school graduation, Elnora was asked to play the violin solo "Méditation" from Thaïs by Jules Massenet. Whenever she played a solo, Elnora liked her parents to get her a new dress. She liked looking pretty, and thought if she looked nice the audience would forgive any mistakes she might make. On the Sunday before graduation at the baccalaureate ceremony, she tuned her violin and left it backstage. When she returned to get her violin to play the solo, all the strings were down and the bridge was down, too. Somebody had loosened the pegs. With her absolute pitch, she quickly re-tuned the violin and performed the solo, but on graduation night she left a friend to guard it so it wouldn't happen again.

It was 1938. Elnora was a high school graduate and ready to pursue the next level of music making.

ELNORA STILL ENJOYS A NEW DRESS. THIS ONE WAS FOR A TRAVERSE SYMPHONY ORCHESTRA EVENT, HONORING ELNORA IN 2002

ELNORA'S
COLLEGE PHOTO

PART II

College and Music Teaching

CHICAGO

Elnora applied to Northwestern University in Chicago and the music department accepted her. The Lombardys knew that Northwestern had one of the best music schools, and since Elnora did not want to travel abroad, they urged her to attend Northwestern. She never looked at any other schools, but gladly followed their advice. Her sister Muffi had already gone off to St. Mary's College, a Catholic women's college in Winona, Minnesota.

The trip from Chisholm to Chicago took one and a half days. Elnora and her mother made the journey together, first taking a train from Chisholm to another station in Minnesota, and then more than one bus to reach Chicago. Once she was settled in Evanston, at Northwestern University's campus, her mother continued on by train to visit her brothers in Indiana. It was late afternoon when her mother left her alone in the big city of Chicago. Elnora walked to the shores of Lake Michigan and cried and cried. Then she went back to her room and hugged her violin. She played for a while and then slept. That was the worst of her homesickness. The next morning she got involved in classes and met students who loved music as much as she did.

Elnora dove right into life at Northwestern: quartets, symphony, performances, and accompaniment. She also took private lessons in both piano and violin. Because of her absolute pitch, Elnora was allowed to skip several classes devoted to ear training, but she concentrated hard on her music studies as a double major in piano and violin.

1938 POSTCARD OF NORTHWESTERN UNIVERSITY

A big joy were the Wa-mu shows at Northwestern. These were stage performances with dancing and singing. Elnora played in the orchestra for Wa-mu shows and loved them, and her friend Lloyd Norlin wrote the lyrics for many of the shows. She wasn't the only one who liked the Wa-mu energy and talent. Fred Waring, "America's Singing Master," came every year to spot talent and often picked out singers and dancers to perform with him.

Given the distance, her parents never visited Northwestern during her college years. They wrote letters, which took about eight days to receive, nothing like the instant communication today. She frequently thought of her parents during concerts and rehearsals. "I had my music," said Elnora. "My parents were always with me in my music."

The first year, she lived on campus in a hall that housed music majors. As a sophomore, she joined the Alpha Gamma Delta sorority. Many musicians were part of that sorority, so she enjoyed immediate camaraderie. They dined at their sorority house with fraternity boys waiting on the tables to earn money. The girls discovered it was a fun way to get to know the boys and to be asked on dates.

Besides classes, Elnora was busy earning money through a variety of jobs during college. She auditioned successfully for an accompanist position, and became one of Northwestern's accompanists who got paid to play for rehearsals and to accompany soloists. Since she liked fashion, she got a job modeling in a downtown Chicago hotel and also at the Wieboldts Department Store in Evanston. "I thought I'd like to be a model and have all those pretty clothes," she said. Modeling was fun, and the job gave her such a good discount on clothing that Elnora began to wear her white blouses just once. "Instead of washing them, I'd throw them away and get a new one. Can you imagine?"

Elnora would travel home to Minnesota for Christmas vacation, often getting a ride with another student from Chisholm. One time they got snowbound on the drive home, when Elnora was sharing a ride with her friend, Walter. Walter went to school at Dartmouth College. He picked up Elnora in Evanston on his way home from Dartmouth, but they were forced to stay overnight in Wisconsin because of a huge snowstorm. In those days, young men and young women did not spend the night together, and Elnora was afraid the event would raise eyebrows.

During her junior year, Elnora took the train from Chisholm to California to see her sister, Muffi. It was a long journey, including two nights sleeping on the train. The train was full of Navy Seabees. When the Seabees saw Elnora with her violin they said: "Why don't you play your violin?" So Elnora obligingly took out her violin and played for them. Soon they were all singing patriotic songs together. One Seabee was so struck by Elnora and her music that he said: "I want to send you to my mother in Florida."

On summer breaks, Elnora returned home to work with her parents in the garden and help out at the farmers market. However, the summer before her junior year she worked as a counselor at Camp Northwoods, a summer camp for girls from Chicago located in Eagle River, Wisconsin. She'd seen an ad in the Chicago newspaper and thought being a music teacher for girls in Eagle River sounded like fun.

She was accepted, and then had to figure out how to get to Eagle River, which involved taking a train from Duluth to Eagle River. Elnora fell asleep on the train and got off at the wrong place, in Rhinelander. She had to wait for the next train to Eagle River. When Elnora finally arrived, the counselors greeted her, showed her where to stay, and immediately gave her a camp nickname. "We'll call you 'Matie,'" they said.

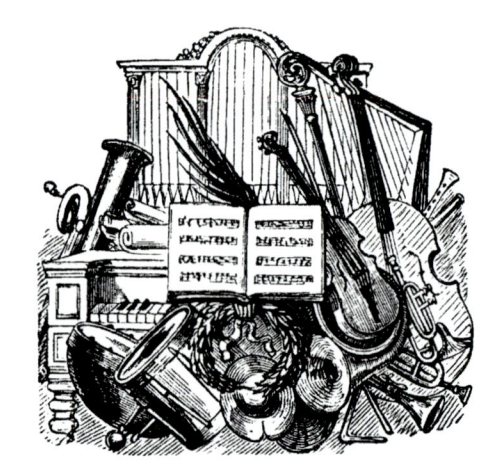

That first night at Camp Northwoods was an adventure. The counselors had told her that if girls had to go to the latrine during the night, they would knock on her door so she could help them. Elnora's boyfriends from Chisholm had jokingly warned her ahead of time about the "bears and wolves," and to expect plenty of wildlife in Eagle River. That very night a girl knocked on the door in the middle of the night to use the bathroom. Elnora looked out. Looking past the girl, she saw a black thing. "A bear! That's a bear!" she cried, and screamed. Her screams woke the whole camp. It turned out to be the camp owner's dog.

At Camp Northwoods, most of the girls were from Chicago and other parts of Illinois. They all called Elnora "Matie," and as their music counselor Elnora led them in songs, did dramatics and taught piano and other instruments. She was nervous around big horses, so when the girls were riding horses she rode a pony. They all slept together in cabins with mosquitoes but still had good times, including bathing beauty contests.

Nearby the camp was a dance club, and the camp owner suggested Elnora try out for the dance band. She took her violin concerto, which she was practicing for her music degree, to try out. They said, "Oh, no. We don't want you to play a concerto. We want you to play a dance band song." So she auditioned on "My Sister and I," a popular song. The song was easy to play compared to a concerto, so she got hired right away. After that, Elnora played with the dance band three times a week and made $500 by the end of the season. She put the money toward college, and, following her mother and father's advice, sewed it in her bra for safekeeping.

Back at Northwestern, Elnora had decided to pursue a teaching certificate so she could be a music teacher. During her junior year she became a student teacher and was chosen to travel to a black section of Evanston. This was a junior high school with students up to ninth grade. She taught violin, viola, cello and string bass once a week. The students had been playing for many years already and had excellent skills and rhythm. "It was a thrill to be with the students, how quickly they caught on. They were so musical," said Elnora. However, not everyone at that time was thrilled. Racial attitudes were slowly evolving. Sometimes when Elnora returned from teaching in Evanston her sorority roommates would ask her to change her clothes. Other times she caused a stir by having a Coke at the drugstore with a fellow student, a string bass player who was black. "In music I was used to all colors," she said. "Music is about human feelings."

DETROIT, APRIL 1942. JACK DELANO,
PHOTOGRAPHER. FSA-OWI COLLECTION.
PRINTS & PHOTOGRAPHS DIVISION,
LIBRARY OF CONGRESS

DETROIT

*E*lnora graduated from Northwestern in 1942 with a music major in piano and violin. In her senior year, Elnora already had nine credits toward her master's degree and had been offered a position teaching music in Des Plaines, Illinois. One day, John Beattie, dean of the Music School at Northwestern, called Elnora and said: "Elnora, Detroit is crying for string teachers."

"But Dean Beattie, I already have a position in Des Plaines," answered Elnora.

"Detroit is crying for string teachers," he repeated. "I'm sending eight of you there, and you're one of them."

Elnora was ready for the adventure. Eight young music teachers from Northwestern set out for Detroit and met with the Detroit school board for three days. Only two of the eight were accepted, and one of them was Elnora. "Nobody was chosen from the University of Michigan!" exclaimed Elnora.

After being hired, Elnora didn't know where to stay. Detroit had several boarding houses located in beautiful homes that took in college students and single people. "Would you like the House of Lenz or the House of Anderson?" they asked her. She chose the House of Lenz, and lived there very happily for two years, her entire time in Detroit.

Her very first assignment was as a string teacher in an all-black Detroit neighborhood. She had enjoyed working with black students before, in Evanston, but this district scared her. It was in a poverty-stricken section of town, and she was intimidated by the school security guard who wanted to date her. Elnora went to see Mr. Smith, the head of the music program, and told him how unhappy she was. Mr. Smith was a stern, intimidating man, and everyone was afraid of him. She cried all the way back to her room at the House of Lenz.

However, one day, shortly thereafter, the principal announced: "Miss Toldo, you are no longer here." Oh, no! Elnora thought. I've been fired, and after only two weeks! Instead the principal went on: "You are to report to the Arthur Robinson district." This was the best school district in Detroit, and included five schools. All the other teachers were jealous of her good fortune and refused to talk to her. Elnora was amazed, and thankful that speaking up had worked. "I learned from that to feel positive about yourself and don't let people walk all over you," she said. She switched to the Arthur Robinson district right away. She loved teaching there, and stayed at Arthur Robinson throughout her time as a music teacher in Detroit. The House of Lenz provided a lovely home for Elnora. Both young men and women boarded there, and the landlady served dinner downstairs in the dining room. Elnora shared one room with three roommates, including a friend named Vivian. Because of the war, the women outnumbered the men. The few men boarding there were mostly students or 4-Fs, men officially designated not fit for military service. One day Elnora said to her friend, "There isn't a man in this House worth looking at twice!"

"There's John Milliken," replied Vivian. "He's in medical school and his father is a state senator. You might like him."

"When does he dine?" asked Elnora.

Two weeks passed before she got a chance to meet John. The House of Lenz boarders dined at small tables, four people to a table, and they began the meal by introducing themselves. Vivian pointed John out in a fit of giggles. The night they were first introduced, Elnora was dressed in her Northwestern colors, purple and white, and was sitting at the dining room table so straight that John thought she was quite tall until she stood up.

Elnora began to think she'd like to see more of John, but he was always studying. He was the only man with a single room at the House of Lenz, and his room was on the way down to the laundry room in the basement. Elnora used to stumble as she went by his room, and John would poke his head out and say, "May I help you?" "Oh, I'm just going down to press my dickey," Elnora would reply, clutching the little white collar she wore under her sweater. She liked to iron it to look sharp.

Before long John asked her to play ping-pong in the House of Lenz and soon they were enjoying golf, tennis, bicycling and dancing together. Sometimes they would double date with John's friend,

'Men are the greatest creatures created by God'

Dave Wynkoop, who was a lieutenant in the navy. Dave had a convertible, and Elnora would arrange a date for Dave, with the girls sitting in the back and the boys up front. If Dave didn't like his date, he wouldn't talk to her. But most nights they all got along, and loved driving with the roof rolled back. One night when it began to rain, John said, "Let's stay in the rain!" Dave laughed and said, "I'm only taking orders from John." They all got soaked.

Elnora loved telling John about her days in Chisholm. When she told him about the time she'd slept in a tree as a Girl Scout, and had tied all the knots herself, he didn't believe her. "You never did that!" he said.

World War II was on, but did not affect their lives much. As a medical student, John was not expected to sign up for service. His skills would be used later, when he had earned his medical degree. Elnora was focused on John and her music. "It was a bad time because of the war, but it was a good time because I met John," said Elnora. "When you're that age, nothing else matters." Years later, in 1972, Elnora said in an interview with the Traverse City Record-Eagle: "Men are the greatest creatures created by God. What a lonely world this world would be without them."

While Elnora was dating John, Elnora's sister Muffi also came to live at the House of Lenz. She had been working at the Mayo Clinic in Minnesota, and had married Charles Lawler after college. Now her husband was in the service fighting in Europe, and while he was away she moved to Detroit and found a job working for a doctor.

When November came, John invited Elnora to his parents' home in Traverse City for Thanksgiving. Elnora asked her parents what to do since she was still dating other young men besides John. "Thanksgiving is a family affair," they told her. "You shouldn't go unless you are very interested." Elnora declined the invitation. By the next Thanksgiving, they were married.

When Elnora had gone on dates in Chicago with her boyfriend Lloyd, he had always presented her with a corsage and a poem about her. She mentioned this to John. He began giving her a corsage also, but no poem. When Easter came, a white box arrived. Expecting a corsage, Elnora opened the box, and then screamed when she saw a live rabbit inside, with pink eyes and a pink ribbon around his neck. Her roommates were delighted, and together they found a basket and straw for the bunny. They kept the rabbit for a week at the House of Lenz until the landlady discovered their pet and reminded them of the house rules: no animals. "I can still see that pink ribbon and those pink eyes looking up at me," said Elnora.

At one point, John decided to briefly move out of the House of Lenz because he needed more time for quiet study before exams. "Instead of studying, we'd go out dancing," said Elnora. John's grades suffered. After the exams, one of John's professors called John into his office and said, "Milliken, no matter which way I turn it, you come out with a D+, but you wrote such an excellent paper that I'll give you a C-." Exams over, John moved back to his regular room at the House of Lenz.

John proposed during a dinner date at a downtown Detroit restaurant. "He had me slip my hand under the tablecloth and he put the ring on." She was thrilled, surprised and shaken when she saw the beautiful ring. The waiter brought them champagne to celebrate, and they toasted to their good fortune in finding each other.

John and Elnora were married on June 24, 1944. Carl Grawn, John's uncle, hosted the wedding at

ELNORA WITH JOHN'S MOTHER,
HILDEGARDE GRAWN MILLIKEN

his house in Grosse Pointe, Michigan. Muffi, Elnora's sister, was maid of honor. John's parents and his sister, Ruthie, came. His brother, Bill, could not attend since he was in the service in Europe. Elnora's parents also could not attend. Her mother wasn't well, and her father didn't want to leave her.

Elnora and John honeymooned on Mackinac Island. Since John had grown up riding horses, the Mackinac cab driver let him take the reins of the horse and buggy. They stayed at a hotel with a piano in the lobby, and Elnora played every day. Thirty years later, John and Elnora returned to the same hotel on Mackinac Island. The man at the desk said, "Weren't you the one who played piano on your honeymoon?"

MACKINAW ISLAND AND THE GRAND HOTEL

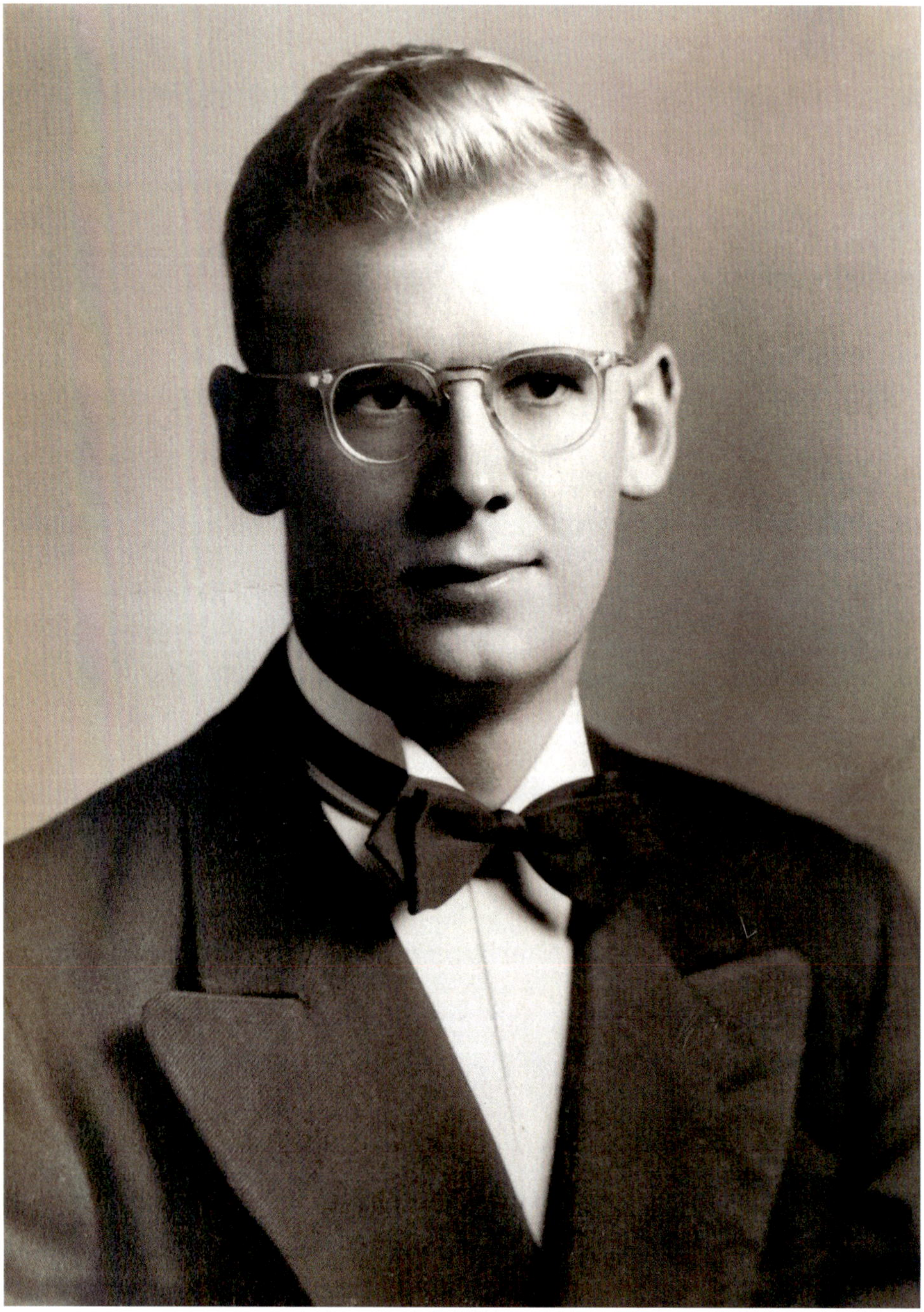

PART III

MARRIED LIFE

DR. JOHN

John Milliken knew from fifth grade that he wanted to be a doctor.

When he was growing up during the Great Depression, there were only about three or four doctors in Traverse City. His family was friends with one of them, a man named Dr. George Coleman, who used to travel by bus from Chicago up to Traverse City to see patients. Young Dr. John developed a great respect for the medical profession, partly due to Dr. Coleman.

By high school, his interest in medicine had grown and he became an x-ray technician in his junior year. There was only one x-ray machine in Traverse City, and it was located at the Traverse City State Hospital, the psychiatric asylum in town. John and one other man were the only people who knew how to operate the x-ray machine. "The other was a psychopathic patient, also named John," said Dr. John. When doctors needed an x-ray, they'd track down one of the Johns; sometimes teenaged Dr. John would be at the movie theater when they called him to come help with x-rays.

John Milliken was born on January 30, 1920. His parents traveled to Detroit for the birth because his mother wanted the benefit of nitrous oxide and the Detroit hospital had the capability to provide it. "I'm a native of Traverse City except for three days," Dr. John liked to tell people.

The Milliken family had lived in Traverse City since the 1800s. On his mother's side, Dr. John's grandfather was Charles Grawn, a prominent school superintendent in the area who had emigrated from Sweden with his parents when he was just a baby. The town of Grawn, nine miles south of Traverse City, was named for him. John's grandfather on his father's side, James Wheelock Milliken, of Scottish descent, left Maine as a young man and arrived in Traverse City to work as a laborer for the Hannah & Lay Mercantile Company in the 1870s. He began a dry goods and clothing business with a friend, and it later became the Milliken's department store. James went on to become a State senator, and he and his wife, Callie Thacker, had one son. John never met his grandfather Milliken. He died on a train from a sudden heart attack at age fifty, while en route to see his only son, John's father, graduate from Yale.

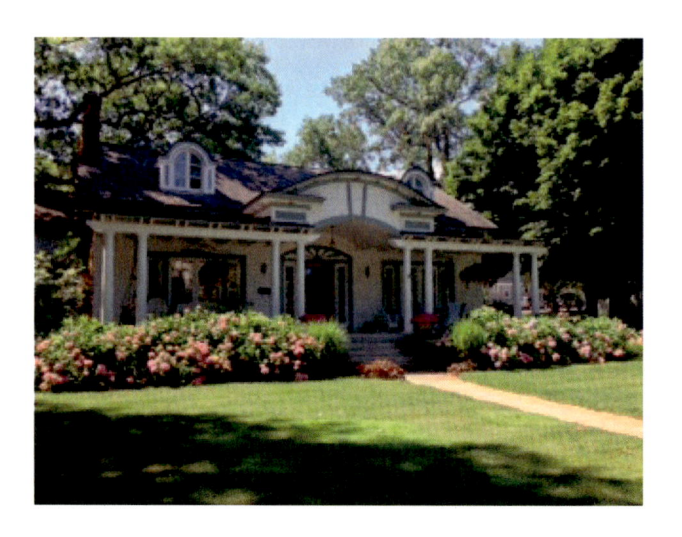

THE FORMER MILLIKEN HOUSE ON WASHINGTON STREET, WHERE JOHN GREW UP

The Milliken family was deeply involved in politics and business. John's father, James Thacker Milliken, became Traverse City's mayor and also served as a State senator. His mother, Hildegarde Grawn, actively campaigned for women's right to vote. Later, John's brother, Bill, became governor of Michigan from 1969-1983. A Republican like his father and grandfather, Bill's socially progressive leadership style became popularly known throughout Michigan by the term "Milliken Republican."

"I am the only doctor in a family of politicians and business people," said Dr. John.

Dr. John's childhood home was 504 Washington Street, on the southeast corner of Washington and Wellington. He was the oldest of three children, with a younger brother, Bill, and sister, Ruth. John loved riding his horse, King High, and sailing on the bay.

The family owned a cottage nearby in Acme. John and his siblings delighted in playing there. The land had its own stream running through it and included 1200 feet of shoreline on East Grand Traverse Bay, land that is now part of the Grand Traverse Resort. As children, they would collect old bottles in a local barnyard and give them to their mother, who ran an antique shop. They sold the bottles for ten cents, and sometimes could sell them to wealthy people for five dollars.

John's mother made friends with Mrs. Ogden Armour who summered on Long Lake. The Armour family owned a meat packing business and was a leader in the industry. Every summer Mrs. Armour traveled up to her summer estate with an entourage of twenty-five helpers. She even had her own rail car. "Mother would often stay with her in Chicago," said Dr. John. "For Christmas, the family gave us barrels of Armour's best preserves. The glasses they came in were so beautiful, we kept them for our regular glasses."

As young teens, John and his brother would spend the night in a smaller two-room cabin in Acme near the family's summer house, and then sneak out to Oatka Beach to dance. Oatka was a dance hall right on the beach by Four Mile Road, that became a hot spot for young people in the 1930s.

Dancing wasn't the only secret adventure John got up to. As a teenager, Dr. John loved mischief. He formed the Double B's Club with his brother Bill and some friends. There were about five or six boys in the club, and they took turns being the president. The Club met in the attics of empty houses belonging to people who had gone away for the winter. Since they sneaked in without permission, the Double B's attracted the police several times. The most memorable Club meeting was when Bill was acting as president at the empty Wynkoops' house. Bill was trying to bring the meeting to order by stamping his foot. He stamped so hard he broke a beam and his foot went right through the ceiling of the master bedroom.

Bill and John each had a horse. They decided to go riding with friends where the Mt. Holiday ski area stands today. "There was nothing but trees and forest," said Dr. John. The boys built a rough cabin for themselves, "cutting down about a hundred trees to do so." They built a corral next to the cabin for their horses. One day the boys heard a shout nearby, and they panicked, worried about being caught. Dr. John yelled "Get on your horses and get out of here!" They rode away and the Double B's stopped going to the cabin.

Besides mischief-making adventures with his friends, John liked music and athletics. He attended Traverse City High School located on Seventh Street. He played violin in the school orchestra and was on the school basketball and track teams, earning six letters total and playing —and almost winning — the state basketball championships. John also dipped his foot in local politics as a boy. His high school created an office for student governor, and John won the election to become the school's first student governor. "I found out one of the benefits was I didn't have to go to study hall," said John. Later, John continued to stay active in local politics, serving on the Traverse City city commission and local boards.

Starting at age fourteen, John worked at the family department store and also worked in a family-owned factory. This was a factory started by John's grandfather. Besides founding Milliken's department store, James Wheelock Milliken had also started a factory in Traverse City that built seeding tools for farmers to plant corn and potatoes. Later the business diversified into building radios and producing pesticide sprayers and became known as the Acme Line Manufacturing Company.

"One of the things I did in the factory was to put a BB in the check valve and take a hammer and hit it. I had to do this many times per hour," said John. He also brought his own brand of mischief to the factory.

"In those days the radios had tubes and coils," said John. "I found out that if you wound the coils a certain way, you could jam the radio signals throughout the neighborhood. I was so thrilled." There was only one radio station in town then. "I got a certain pleasure from being able to cut off reception for about a mile. I even received a letter from the federal government to cease and desist."

After high school graduation in 1938, John headed east to attend Amherst College. "Don't ask me how I got in, because I don't know," he said. Many of his friends had gone to prep schools and had been preparing for college entrance for years. His first exam was history with Professor Packer, and John was anxious about the results. "I was so nervous during the exam that I could barely read my writing, yet I was the only one with straight A's. From then on I felt no insecurity." John played freshman basketball at Amherst and joined the Chi Psi fraternity.

John applied to medical school early. Some students were doing this to avoid being drafted in World War II, but that wasn't John's reason. After knowing his career passion since fifth grade, John was eager to get going, so he applied to thirty medical schools. "I didn't want to get out of the draft, I wanted to be a physician." He was the only one from his Amherst classmates to be accepted to medical school during his junior year.

To aid his quest in becoming a doctor, John took his old convertible and drove to many of the medical schools he applied to. One stop was Loyola University in Chicago. He found out where the medical school dean lived, and drove his convertible to the dean's house, knocking on his door at eight o'clock on a Sunday morning. "Instead of throwing me out, he spent three hours interviewing me." John got accepted by Loyola, and also by others, but he selected Wayne State University. John chose Wayne State because it was one of the most practical schools. The medical school had seventy students. He would have the chance to do surgery and he liked its downtown Detroit location.

Luckily he did, or he might never have met Elnora.

John was so eager to start medical school that he began his studies at Wayne State before finishing his undergraduate degree. So John left Amherst in 1941, one year before graduation, and moved into Detroit's House of Lenz. He received his B.S. degree from Amherst at a later date.

EARLY MARRIED LIFE

After their wedding, John and Elnora moved to Dallas, Texas in 1944. At long last, John had officially become Dr. John. He had graduated from medical school that spring with a specialty in internal medicine. His first placement was an internship at Baylor University Hospital in Dallas. The new couple rented an apartment and settled in for the first months of married life.

Baylor was a big hospital with about twenty-five interns. Some of John's work involved working in the obstetric wing delivering babies. He also performed regular surgeries, sometimes substituting for the main doctor at the last minute.

DALLAS, TEXAS. 1944

One day as he entered the operating room, John saw a woman lying on the operating table ready for a uterine tumor to be removed. Dr. Shertel told him, "Milliken, I'm pretty tired. You do it." Dr. John went on to perform about half the doctor's surgeries under his supervision. As his internship period was drawing to a close, Dr. Shertel said to John: "Milliken, I'm sorry to see you leave my service. Today, I'm going to be your assistant. See how fast you can get the gall bladder out." Surgery then was not laparoscopic; it involved opening the whole abdomen. In thirteen minutes, John had cut through the abdomen, removed the gall bladder and sewed the patient back up satisfactorily.

Meanwhile, Elnora was playing music and planning for their future family. She joined the Dallas symphony, and continued playing and attending rehearsals when she became pregnant with their first child. One rainy evening when the orchestra was in the middle of playing Tchaikovsky's Fifth Symphony, Elnora didn't feel well. She called John and said, "I think something's happening." John drove her straight to the hospital. Their daughter Sherry arrived that night, born six weeks early.

Dr. John assisted with his own daughter's birth. The umbilical cord was wrapped around her neck and John knew the doctor on duty was nervous, so John came in to help with the delivery. Despite being an early baby, Sherry was strong and never needed to be put in an incubator.

Elnora loved life in Texas. "I wanted to stay in Texas. I loved it there," she said. But John couldn't get used to Texas, including cement-bottomed swimming pools. Having grown up surrounded by the beautiful sandy beaches of northern Michigan, John said: "I cannot swim where there's a cement bottom." His father echoed the sentiment: "There's no place as beautiful as Traverse City. You must come back home."

When the Texas internship ended, Elnora and John drove north with baby Sherry. It wasn't time to return to Traverse City yet, but it was time for family visits. They drove more than 1,000 miles from Dallas to Chisholm, Minnesota. It was winter and "only" 30° F below zero. Elnora had her fur collar coat but John was unprepared for the cold. This was the first time Elnora had seen her parents since she had been married, and the first chance John had had to meet Elnora's parents. Peter and Lucia changed out of their gardening overalls and dressed up in their best clothes for the occasion. "My father looked so handsome. He liked to dress up," said Elnora. She proudly introduced them to their first granddaughter.

After Dallas, the family moved briefly back to Detroit, where John had a residency at the Alexander Blaine Clinic for nine months, and then on to Battle Creek for two years. Their son Jim, or James Grawn Milliken, was born in 1946 in Battle Creek. Now Elnora had her hands full, since Jim was born soon after Sherry.

In Battle Creek, John worked as a psychiatrist for the U.S. Army Medical Corps at Percy Jones Hospital. He'd completed basic training in El Paso while they lived in Texas. John was assigned to serve the war effort with his medical knowledge as a medical officer for the Army. The war was winding down, but the need for psychiatric services was increasing as soldiers who had been stationed overseas returned home. Many soldiers suffering from war trauma were sent to Battle Creek for treatment. John served under Captain Jerry Adaiman, a well-known psychiatrist. "In those days, treatment of mental patients was different. We did frontal lobotomies," said John. Altogether Dr. John served as a medical officer for two years, from 1946 to 1948.

Their first apartment in Battle Creek had thin walls and an iron stove for heat. John bought a folding hide-a-bed to furnish the apartment. After a while they rented a house in Battle Creek while John finished his work at Percy Jones. "John was so helpful," said Elnora. "I couldn't stand to wash the diapers, and he always did the diapers downstairs in the old house." Friends would stop by and ask: "where's John?" He'd be down in the basement washing diapers.

Elnora used to be afraid of being left alone in the Battle Creek house when John had to work at night. Sometimes she heard footsteps on the front porch. It turned out there was a window peeper in the neighborhood who was finally caught. John arranged for a young woman to stay with Elnora on nights when she would be alone. The arrangement didn't last: the woman he hired snored and told vivid stories that scared Elnora even more.

When John was discharged from his medical military service, their next move was to Ann Arbor where John had a residency at the University of Michigan's University Hospital. He was placed in psychiatry at University of Michigan, too, although his main love remained internal medicine. John and family lived in Pittsfield Village.

Wherever they went, Elnora found a symphony, or sometimes two or three. In Detroit, she'd played with the Detroit Teacher's Symphony. While living in Battle Creek, she played not only in the Battle Creek Symphony, but also the Kalamazoo Symphony and the Jackson Symphony. While the family lived in Pittsfield Village, Elnora joined the Ann Arbor Symphony. She played in string quartets, too. The cellist in the Battle Creek quartet had the odd practice of painting the room before the quartet practiced in her house. Every time they came, she painted. "Can you imagine?" said Elnora. "I couldn't stand the fumes, they made me feel sick, but she was a very good cellist, so I stayed." When she played her music, Elnora hired young girls to look after her children. "I always found time for my music, even though I had young children," she said.

Dr. John soon became an assistant resident in Ann Arbor, and then was promoted to full resident. Dr. Sturgis, the chief of medicine, supervised all thirty-five residents, and promoted John six months ahead of the rest. John was pleased with his new status. "I got to wear a white coat and civilian clothes. I had more time, too." Dr. Sturgis was an internationally respected doctor. He would kid John by saying: "Milliken, I've always wondered about you. Why didn't you go to Michigan? Your grades not good enough?" University of Michigan was one of the top medical schools in the country, and people came from all over the country to attend Dr. Sturgis' medical conferences. Sometimes he picked John to give the opening remarks. "It was an honor to address all those people," said John. By his last year in Ann Arbor he had joined the staff as a full instructor of internal medicine.

TRAVERSE CITY STATE HOSPITAL

PART IV

Home in Traverse City

MILLIKEN MEDICAL BEGINS

It was 1950. Dr. John was thirty years old, with a wife and two children. It was finally time to return home to Traverse City and start practicing medicine.

Traverse City had grown by this time. There were now thirty to forty doctors in town, and the Traverse City State Hospital no longer did frontal lobotomies to treat mentally ill patients. There were only two other doctors of internal medicine; John became the third. Internal medicine doctors at that time trained much longer than they do today.

John first joined a medical practice run by a family friend, Dr. Hall. The partnership didn't last long. After only a month or two together, John noticed that Dr. Hall wasn't referring any of his patients to him, despite being overscheduled. John confronted his partner. "Are you afraid of me?" he asked. "Yes," said Dr. Hall. John moved out and set up his own independent practice.

JOHN'S 700 SQUARE FOOT MEDICAL OFFICE BY THE HOSPITAL BECAME THE MILLIKEN MEDICAL BUILDING WITH 12 BUILDING ADDITIONS AND MORE DOCTORS

His first office was above the Goodyear garage on Front Street. He hired a receptionist he couldn't afford and announced he was accepting new patients. In those early days, John had many "zero" days with no patients. "It was hard. I'll never forget when I got my first patient," he said. By the time John's first patient arrived, he had already turned away his assistant due to lack of funds.

John didn't have much money, but he was full of innovative ideas. To cool the office, John visited the junkyard and brought back a barrel and some radiator equipment. The ice man used to make daily deliveries back then, and John blew a fan over the ice to air condition the office.

Besides keeping office hours, John also made house calls. Doctors were beginning to see more patients in their offices by then, but house calls were still part of the medical practice in the 1950s.

One patient gratefully told him: "You're the only doctor I can call in the middle of the night and you still sound cheerful."

Before long, John was seeing regular patients and he decided to build his own medical building. He chose a field across the street from Munson Hospital and built a white building that is today the Milliken Medical Building. He was the first doctor to build nearby the hospital. The man who sold him the lot said: "Doctor, you're going to buy two lots." John protested that he didn't have the money, but the owner said: "Pay me a nickel down and nickel a month." So John invested in two lots on the site, each costing $2,000. Dr. Lemon followed John's example and bought the land next to his, and soon medical offices were growing around the hospital.

EVERY YEAR, ELNORA PLANTED THE ROSE SOCIETY'S "ROSE OF THE YEAR" OUTSIDE THE MILLIKEN MEDICAL BUILDING

The Milliken Medical Building started with 700 square feet. John got the money he needed from a bank loan, based on his earning potential. The first few years it was a struggle to keep up with the payments, but the Milliken Medical Building turned out to be a good investment. Eventually the building expanded to a nine-physician clinic in a two-story building, with two working elevators, and 22,000 square feet. The Milliken Medical Building became Dr. John's professional home for the next fifty-four years.

Elnora planted roses at the Milliken Medical Building. She loved roses, especially bright pink flowers, and various shades of pink. When John put additions on his office building, including a covered patio, Elnora added roses and tended them carefully. Each year she made sure to plant the Rose Society's "Rose of the Year." She was delighted that patients and doctors could see the roses from the hallway and exam rooms. "If you go to see the doctor and you see flowers, it makes you forget what you're worried about," she explained. "That's why I planted roses there."

Doctor John and Elnora also built the Milliken Inn, located kitty corner to the Milliken Medical Building, right by the hospital. John's idea was that families would need a place to stay when someone was in the hospital, and they would appreciate a pleasant guesthouse nearby. The Milliken Inn had twelve rooms. Elnora chose the color peach for the outside walls, and together she and John picked out the furniture in Florida. "That was so much fun," she said. "We designed it, and ran the inn as a husband and wife team." The Inn got off to a slow start — barely breaking even in the third year — but eventually did well. One time they had nobody available to clean the rooms, so John asked Elnora to clean and make the beds.

Then came a time when Munson Hospital directors talked about moving the hospital to another location. "That was alarming," said John. "For a period there I was pretty heavily mortgaged, and it would've been a catastrophe for me." Munson stayed in its existing location and expanded instead.

Besides his home base at the Milliken Medical Building, John also saw patients in Kingsley, Cadillac, Empire and Manistique. For a year, he also had an office in Kingsley, but business began to slow down there. He charged about twenty dollars for a physical exam. Finally a Kingsley patient said: "Dr. Milliken, do you know why you're not very busy here? Do you know why you're not getting new patients? Because you charge too much." John shut his office in Kingsley and focused on Traverse City. One time a Traverse City woman phoned to cancel her appointment saying: "I just went to your store and bought a new coat. I feel so good I don't need to see you."

John was one of the few local physicians at the time who could read electrocardiograms. He did readings for patients in Kalkaska, Manistee and various parts of the Upper Peninsula. If he was away on a trip attending a medical conference, hospitals would send the electrocardiograms to the nearest post office marked "General Delivery." Elnora would help him by typing his reports, and she always traveled with a manual typewriter just in case. John called her the queen of typing speed. "I loved to type. I could type 120 words a minute. Playing the violin and piano, my fingers were agile," said Elnora.

John worked long hours as a doctor. On days he worked in Cadillac, he would sometimes get home at 2am after seeing critically ill patients at Cadillac's Mercy Hospital for twelve hours. Dr. John liked to be on the cutting edge of medical progress. His was the first local clinic to have x-ray and lab services on-site, and was the first doctor's office to use computers.

Just as John was starting his own practice, he was called to help the family business, the Acme Line Manufacturing Company. The company had been thriving with five buildings and up to 400 employees, but when John and Elnora returned from Ann Arbor, the company was limping along with eighty employees and facing bankruptcy. John took charge of the company, along with a friend, and got it back on its feet.

AN ACME LINE SPRAYER

John said: "I remember picking up the telephone and calling the administrator, asking: 'Did you pay for that part?' Because if we didn't it would shut our assembly line down." John attended sales meetings and got actively involved in the factory until he was able to sell it to a new buyer. Although the factory took enormous time, it also proved to be a blessing. "I was fortunate," said John. "Half of the factory became my patients. It helped me survive and get established in my practice."

It was while John was involved in Acme Line Manufacturing that he met Les Biederman, founder of the Northwestern Michigan College. Les's car was stuck in the snow, and John helped push him out. They struck up a friendship, and John invited Les to join the board of the Acme Line company. Les was in the radio business and had an eighth grade education, but he was brilliant. As a board member, Les helped promote the Acme Line sprayers and negotiated airtime on WWO a big TV station in New York. Les flew out to New York on a propeller driven DC-3 with the sprayers strapped to his back. The idea was to do a live demonstration on TV, but when he arrived, for some reason the sprayers jammed and wouldn't work. Les quickly bought two sprayers from a competitor's brand, peeled off the Acme Line labels and stuck them on to the competitor's models just in time to go on the air. The Acme Line Manufacturing Co. sold 500 sprayers in a minute.

*J*ohn also served on the Traverse City city commission for four years beginning in 1961. The most significant vote he made as a commissioner concerned the commission's decision to build a new coal-fired power plant right on the shores of West Grand Traverse Bay. This was one of the city's greatest controversies. John cast the lone vote against building the power plant at that location. "Someday you'll regret it," he told the commission. He could see the potential of the waterfront for future uses, and sure enough, forty years later the city tore down the power plant and transformed the land into public parkland.

John and Elnora were not involved in Bill Milliken's political life as governor. Bill and Helen kept very busy, and John and Elnora did, too, so the two families got together mainly at holiday gatherings.

CLOCKWISE:
ELNORA, JOHN, JIM,
SHERRY AND WENDY

PENINSULA DRIVE

When the John Milliken family moved to Traverse City they rented a house on State Street where they lived as a family of four for two years. The house had three bedrooms. John's mother Hildegarde gave them a beautiful black dining room table and chairs, and they bought new carpet and a washing machine. The washing machine, however, had a bad habit of flooding, because it sat on a slanting kitchen floor.

They chose to build a permanent home on West Bay around 1953. John found land on Peninsula Drive, and Elnora and John designed the house with the help of an architect. They designed a modern contemporary house with floor to ceiling picture windows in the living room to overlook the bay. Elnora wanted to enlarge the living room by ten feet during construction to fit two baby grand pianos for performing, but in the end they kept the living room the same size. Both Elnora and John wanted to incorporate the outdoors wherever they could. John's original idea was to build a water dock under the house so he could sail his boats right in. That didn't happen either, but he did have his boats in front of the house. Elnora cried when they had to cut some beautiful birch trees on the side of the house.

To build their dream house, Elnora and John had to travel to Grand Rapids to get a special building loan. "How much is this going to cost?" Elnora asked her husband. Traverse City's banking business was growing, but no one did loans like that at the time. The finished house was 2,300 square feet. Later they added a tennis court and boat dock down by the bay, as well as additions. "We had so many friends, we added two guest houses," said Elnora.

Meanwhile, their family was growing. Wendy Joan Milliken was born in 1955 and Penny Ruth Milliken soon followed in 1957. Four years later John Peter Milliken, or JP, was born in 1961, completing their family. The family also had two German shepherds and one St. Bernard, since John liked dogs. Elnora still maintained her childhood fear of dogs, but because John was gone so much, she felt safe having a German shepherd by the door.

At that time, home delivery was common for milk and groceries. "It was so nice!" said Elnora. "You didn't have to go shopping." However, the milkman hit one of their German shepherds with his milk truck. JP witnessed the accident.

Elnora loved gardening at her new home. She planted raspberries and peonies carefully transported from her parents' garden in Chisholm, Minnesota. The family would often visit Chisholm in the springtime and sometimes the fall, too. Elnora brought her parents local peaches, and they would collect peony bulbs to plant back in Michigan. Some of the peony plants surrounding their Peninsula Drive home are more than a hundred years old.

Elnora loved flower arranging, too, and studied ikebana. She filled the house with light pink, dark pink and white peonies as well as fragrant peach blossoms when the peach trees were in bloom. For a time, she had two peach trees by the house, but John had to cut them down to improve the road down to the beach.

CHILDREN AND MUSIC

The Milliken family was an active, cheerful household. John liked the children's rooms to be neat. "I would always say 'Your father's coming home. Put everything under the bed!'" said Elnora.

Each Sunday, the family went to church at Immaculate Conception, followed by breakfast at a local restaurant, usually the Pinestead Reef. They went skiing, ice skating, boating, swimming and played tennis and music together. One favorite skating rink was by Thirlby field, the football field on Fourteenth Street, and another was by the bay where the Senior Center now stands. Elnora and John used to love taking the children downhill skiing at Boyne Mountain. "We'd take the children out of school Wednesday night and they'd ski all day Thursday," said Elnora. "Can you do that anymore?"

One time the family invited a big group of friends to come over for skiing at Siebold Hill. Elnora made a big pot of spaghetti chili. It was a beautiful day. John was ahead of Elnora on the rope tow, and children were pulling on it, which caused Elnora to land on her stomach with her leg turned out. She'd broken two bones in her leg. She needed a plate put in and was on crutches for many months after that bad skiing accident.

Since it was difficult to look after children with a bad leg, they hired help, including a woman named Dorothy. One day when John was seeing patients in Cadillac and Elnora was laid up with her crutches, Dorothy said she would take little Jim out and go shopping. Jim was three years old at the time. They left mid-afternoon, but by 6pm still had not returned. Elnora called her brother-in-law Bill, who was working nearby at Milliken's Department Store. He discovered Dorothy on Front Street. She was at the Sail Inn drinking and giving little Jim nickels in the bar. Jim came home with pockets full of nickels.

Music was part of Elnora's daily life. She taught all her children to play piano, and delighted when they expressed musical interest. Young Wendy used to play a little child-sized piano when her mother practiced. "When I played piano she would go and sit and play in the living room next to me." Elnora's mother-in-law, Hildegarde, also loved music and gave Elnora an upright Steinway, one

LEFT TO RIGHT: ELNORA, JIM, SHERRY, JOHN. IN FRONT, JP AND PENNY

of the first upright Steinways ever made. Elnora had it painted white. Elnora and Hildegarde used to go to the Ann Arbor music festival together and Hildegarde invited Elnora to perform at lunches and bridge parties around Traverse City. Years later, a music shop in Chicago wanted to buy Elnora's upright Steinway, but instead she kept it and moved it to the family's guest house.

Soon Elnora became known for her music. When a doctor asked her to teach his grandchildren, one child on the piano and one on the violin, it launched her as a music teacher. Within three weeks Elnora had twenty-five music students.

She taught lessons in Guest House #1. Elnora taught violin and piano, and often had more violin students. She held lessons right after school, charging five dollars for a half hour lesson. She liked to start children at about age eight or nine, and if they didn't practice she would dismiss them. Elnora knew that music demanded practice. "I couldn't stand teaching if they didn't practice what I wrote down," she said. Elnora conducted lessons during the school year and held recitals. Most of her students were children, but she also taught a few adults. People were eager to have her; there weren't many music teachers in the area then. Elnora taught private music lessons for forty years.

LEFT TO RIGHT, TOP ROW: ELNORA, JOHN, SHERRY, JIM BOTTOM ROW: JP AND PENNY

ELNORA AND JP

Sherry played piano, and delighted in giving ballet lessons to local children. She also held her ballet class in Guest House #1. Sherry was also an excellent student, coming number one in her graduating class. "I'm not the smartest in my grade," Sherry would tell her mother, "but I know the right way to study." Jim played clarinet. He surprised his mother when she showed up for his concert and saw him sitting in first chair. "He never told me he was first chair," said Elnora. "Jim was quite a musician." Among the younger children, Wendy loved music and playing on her child-sized piano. Penny played piano and violin and was an active singer in school musicals and a member of Madrigals and Choralaires. JP started on trumpet, but switched to baritone after he got braces. The children all loved to stage plays at home, the older ones frequently dressing up JP in funny costumes.

ELNORA WITH DAUGHTER PENNY AND SON JP IN 1972

WENDY'S SONG

Wendy adored music, had a great sense of humor and loved being part of whatever the rest of the family was doing. She was tall for her age and enthusiastic to try everything. At the ice skating rink she'd say: "Daddy, I can't keep up with you!" John could skate backwards, but three-year-old Wendy's little legs could not. She also tried to keep up with her big brother and big sister, Jim and Sherry, who were nine and ten years older.

Sherry delighted in teaching her little sisters to dance. One year she taught Wendy and Penny some ballet to perform at the family's Christmas party. Elnora and John always liked to host a Christmas party at home for their friends. It was 1958. Elnora dressed Wendy and Penny in red dresses with little white pinafores for the occasion.

As Wendy was dancing, John suddenly noticed her lips turned blue. They rushed Wendy down to the hospital in Ann Arbor. On the car ride down, Wendy felt good and amused them with her comments, such as "Mother, there are witches in the bathroom." However, she died in Ann Arbor just after Christmas on December 29th at age three and a half.

Wendy's unexpected death shook the family. Elnora retreated from her friends and family and cried and cried. She cried so much and so long that Sherry said to her: "Mother, if you don't stop crying, Jim and I will think that you don't love the rest of us."

Elnora forced herself to stop crying. "She's right," she thought. "It's not fair to the other children. Wendy will not come back. I have other children and a husband and I should be thankful for what we have." The family helped each other, and frequently went out together to visit Oakwood cemetery where Wendy was buried.

"I saved her little dresses," said Elnora. "And saved a little bit of her hair." What was especially hard was when John confided to Elnora ten years later that advances in medical knowledge meant that Wendy would be alive if doctors had known what they knew now. The news brought fresh grief and anguish. "John knew, but I don't know what she died of," said Elnora. "I never asked."

Wendy's spirit would always be alive in music.

In honor of little Wendy, John took Elnora down to Chicago to choose a piano. They went to Lyon & Healy and picked out a grand piano to go in the living room. "I think of her every time I play it," said Elnora.

She also chose a violin in Wendy's memory. A man came up to Interlochen from Grand Rapids with instruments for sale. Elnora had two violins, her high school one and her college one, but John asked her if she'd like to look at the Interlochen violins. He said: "If you can tell the difference between the instruments, then that's how you should choose it. Choose the one you like the best." John lined the instruments up and blindfolded Elnora with a cloth diaper. She listened for the tone. "It came down to two violins. I kept coming back to one," said Elnora. "I chose the most expensive one. It had a beautiful tone."

More than fifty years later, Elnora still cries when she talks about Wendy. "They're pretty tears for Wendy," she says.

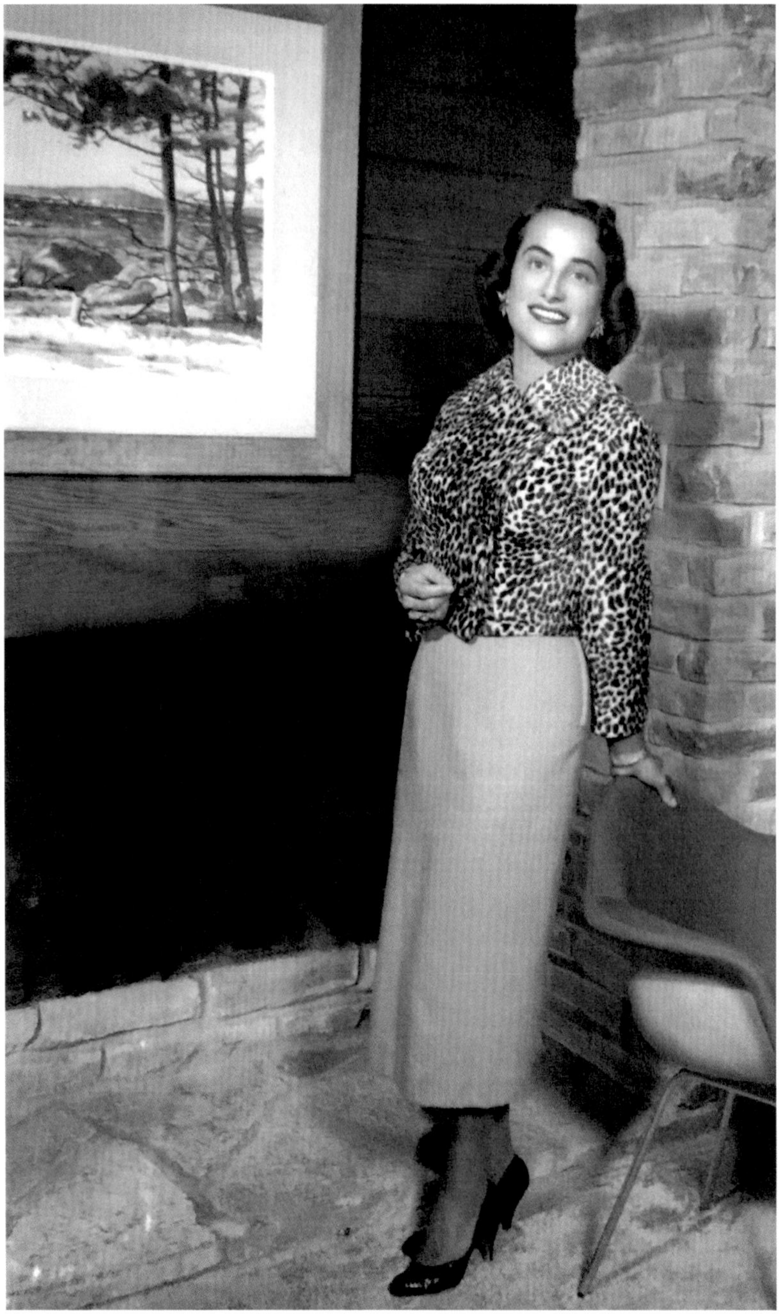

PART V

Arts Pioneer

A TRAVERSE SYMPHONY

When she arrived in Traverse City, Elnora immediately sought out fellow musicians. She joined the Traverse City Musicale, a collection of musicians and music lovers. At the first meeting, she asked: "When does the symphony rehearse?"

The answer shocked her.

"We don't have a symphony," they told her.

"I just about fainted," Elnora said. By then, she'd played in eight symphonies, from the Iron Range symphonies of her childhood — the Hibbing Range Symphony and the Virginia Symphony — to the symphonies of Ann Arbor, Battle Creek, Dallas, Jackson, Kalamazoo and Northwestern University. It didn't seem possible to live in a place without a symphony orchestra. When she got over the shock, Elnora thought to herself: "There's something you can do about this."

Elnora envisioned a symphony for northern Michigan that would draw musicians from Mackinaw City to Traverse City, following the style of the Hibbing Symphony, which had drawn musicians from Duluth to Grand Rapids, Minnesota. Dr. John agreed it was a good idea. At the next Musicale meeting in January 1951, Elnora stood up and announced her bold plan.

"I think we could start a symphony here," she said.

She looked around the room, which was filled with about thirty-five women. Only two raised their hands and offered to help: Louise Williams, a violinist, and Carol Kempton, a cellist. But two was a good start.

Together Elnora and John drew up lists of all the doctors, lawyers, dentists and business people in town. The plan was to ask people for donations of twenty-five, fifty or a hundred dollars. Each day she gave five names to Louise and Carol to contact, and each evening Elnora checked to see what success they'd had. If people didn't say 'yes,' Elnora would add them to her own list. "I had a long list," she said.

When Elnora told people she was forming a symphony, she was often met with blank looks. Some said: "What's that?" They had no idea what a symphony was and had no interest. Many nights after being turned down over and over, Elnora would come home and cry. John would comfort her. "You can't expect everybody to like what you like," he reminded her. Elnora realized the truth in that. Why do I think it's good for everybody? she asked herself. A symphony might not be to everyone's taste, but it would be good for so many people of all ages in Traverse City. She soldiered on.

"If you think it's a good idea, go ahead and pursue it. As long as you are strong in your belief that it's a good thing, then it's good for yourself and the community."

Wherever she went, Elnora talked about the symphony. "When you're excited about something you just talk about it," she said. "People would run away from me at cocktail parties. They'd say – 'Oh no, here comes Elnora! She's going to ask us for money for the symphony.'"

Elnora spent hours on the phone contacting potential supporters and arranging meetings. "You ask my children – I was on the phone night and day, mostly night," Elnora said. When she found a sympathetic ear she'd say: "I want to see you about an important project I have in mind."

One of the first people she called was Dr. Arnold Sarya, who lived across the street from their house. "Well, Elnora, if you think it's good for Traverse City, come at seven o'clock in the morning and bring me my morning paper. While I'm reading the paper, you're welcome to use my sauna. Then come in the house and I'll give you…how much do you want?"

Elnora was thrilled. She loved saunas from her Minnesota days, and after enjoying the sauna's freshness, she decided to be bold and ask for a big amount.

"I'd like a hundred dollars!" she cried. A hundred dollars was worth about a thousand dollars today.

Dr. Sarya gave her the symphony's first gift of a hundred dollars. It was an incredible moment. "To know that someone believed in me," said Elnora. "It made me really believe myself that the symphony would be successful."

The next person she approached was Mr. Powers, brother to Gene Powers. He had an office in the State bank building. Elnora arrived wearing her yellow corduroy raincoat and took the elevator to the top floor. After she explained her idea to form the symphony, Mr. Powers put his glasses down on his desk and looked at her.

"I'm an old man. I don't go out at night," he said.

"Oh! We'll have afternoon concerts, too," she quickly answered.

He looked at her again and smiled. "How much do you want?" he asked.

"A hundred dollars?"

Mr. Powers wrote out a check for one hundred dollars and handed it to Elnora. That was the symphony's second major gift. She was so thrilled she could barely thank him. When she left his office, Elnora held on to the walls because she almost fainted. She couldn't believe that she'd received two gifts of one hundred dollars.

Another person she called early on was Harry Calcutt, a banker who was friends with the Milliken family. She thought he would like culture. When Elnora finished her spiel, Harry said: "Well, I don't know. I don't like symphonies. But if you think it's good for Traverse City, I'll give you ---how much do you want?" Elnora asked for twenty-five dollars. He gave her the twenty-five dollars that day and continued to donate generously to the symphony for many years.

Elnora was unstoppable. "The symphony was on my mind always. I kept telling people we could do it," she said. Elnora first brought the idea to the Musicale group in January 1951. By spring they'd assembled enough players to stage an early concert, led by Dr. Earl Moore, a man who summered in Omena and worked as the Music Department chair at the University of Michigan. The next spring the growing orchestra played again, this time under the direction of Harry Hansen. The concert was free. They called themselves the "Northwestern Michigan Symphony Orchestra of Traverse City" and appeared with the Choral Union. The concert featured two movements from Beethoven's Symphony No. 2 and Haydn's Military Symphony, and the Traverse City Record-Eagle noted the "crispness of the string section," words that pleased Elnora so much.

This was good progress, but Elnora and her symphony friends had their eyes on establishing a proper symphony. They continued fundraising to attract a top conductor who could lead regular rehearsals and present at least three concerts a year. Louise Williams, who'd majored in music at Olivet College, thought of Pedro Paz and invited him to be their conductor. Dr. Paz was a native of Ecuador who had studied in London, Brussels and the Royal Conservatory of Music. At the time, he led the Olivet Symphony and the Jackson Civic Orchestra. He agreed to be the Traverse City symphony conductor.

Pedro Paz arrived in August 1952, traveling up from Olivet once a week to rehearse the new Traverse symphony. They paid him $5,000 a year. All the musicians played for free.

Paz conducted with no baton. "He was a true musician. I fell in love with him," said Elnora. "He made you like him because he liked what he did. He never married; he married music. He drew music out of the players."

Four months later, the orchestra was ready to offer their first concert. The Record-Eagle ran a headline that said: "Musical Housewives Play in N.W. Michigan Symphony Orchestra." Louise Williams was Concert Mistress, with Elnora sitting beside her as Assistant Concert Mistress. About a quarter of the forty-five-member orchestra were housewives like themselves, but the new symphony was a real mix. Some were plumbers, radiologists, power company employees and scrap iron salvage workers. One of the second violin players was a builder who used to come to rehearsals with his nails dirty. Some were self-taught, like Elnora's musical father. Others had taken lessons and played in symphonies in bigger cities. The new orchestra accepted anybody; there were no tryouts. It was composed of musicians from twelve towns, including as far away as Charlevoix and Mackinac Island.

Guest players for the first concert included Joseph Maddy, the founder of Interlochen Center for the Arts, who came up from Ann Arbor with his viola, and his son, Richard Maddy, who played percussion. Other players ranged from the Mayor's wife, Mrs. Nelson, on bassoon, to ninth graders, on trumpet and cello. Carol Kempton had specially gone to the schools and asked music teachers if their advanced students would be interested in joining the symphony. Some came from Interlochen, and some from Traverse City schools.

Elnora held additional rehearsals for string players at her newly built home. They were still completing their house at that time, and didn't have carpeting or doors, but that didn't matter. Music flowed through the open doorways and bare floors. Elnora exhorted the string players to look professional by bowing up and down together. "Follow the concert mistress and mark your music," she said. This was a new concept to many of the musicians who were beginning players and not used to professional symphonies.

To entice new players to join and attend rehearsals, Elnora baked batches of oatmeal raisin cookies. "Where there's food, people will come!" she cried. These cookies were family favorites, cookies she filled with carrots, apples, walnuts, raisins, peanut butter, and buttermilk. "My famous oatmeal raisin cookies had everything in them but the symphony!" said Elnora. Later the Women's Symphony Association provided lunch to feed the musicians, and offered travel money to those who traveled far to reach Traverse City. The orchestra rehearsed in the high school auditorium each week for three years.

For the first concert, Elnora invited high school students to be the ushers and asked the girls to wear their formal dresses. They looked beautiful and excited as they passed out programs for the symphony. The orchestra itself dressed in black and white. Elnora was used to symphonies wearing all black, but wanted to have a brighter look. Milliken's department store gave the players a good discount, and the women ordered white blouses and black skirts from there. The men wore bow ties with their black pants and white shirts.

The symphony's first official concert, with Paz at the helm, was held at 3pm at the high school auditorium on December 21, 1952. The program included: Beethoven's Symphony No. 1 in C Major, Godart's Adagio Pathetique, Suite No. 1 from Carmen by Georges Bizet, and the "Emperor Waltz" by Johann Strauss. Tickets cost one dollar each. "It was amazing!" said Elnora. "People showed up." They did more than show up: the high school auditorium was packed to capacity with an audience of 1,000 people. When Paz stepped down from the podium, the symphony received a long ovation.

The new Traverse symphony had been born.

They celebrated the first concert with a reception at Hildegarde and Jim Milliken's home, inviting all the orchestra players, Pedro Paz, the new symphony board and first donors. The next morning glowing reviews arrived. The concert made the front page of the Grand Rapids Press the next morning. "An Orchestra is Born in Northwestern Michigan" the headline read. "Symphony thrills capacity audience at first concert."

"The first concert with Pedro Paz. That was a symphony," said Elnora. "We acted and played like a real symphony. I was very, very pleased. I thought: This is the beginning. We'll grow and spread our love of music."

The symphony performed three concerts during its first season. By the second concert in March, the orchestra was ready to tackle more ambitious pieces, including Schubert's Overture to Rosamunde, Mozart's Symphony No. 40 in G minor, selections from Tchaikovsky's Nutcracker and Strauss's Perpetuum Mobile. Season tickets for all three concerts were three dollars. At first, adult single tickets cost one dollar and children were fifty cents, but by spring pricing changed so that students were fifty cents and children under twelve were free.

When spring came, Elnora wanted the orchestra to break out of traditional somber black clothing and perform in bright colors. "I wanted us to be colorful like spring flowers," she said. She convinced the women to wear long, colorful dresses for the symphony's first spring concert. Elnora wore pink. Others dressed in green, blue, yellow and white. "I was so happy!" said Elnora. "I felt colorful and happy, so happy with the beautiful music."

THE TRAVERSE SYMPHONY'S FIRST CONCERT WAS PERFORMED ON DECEMBER 21, 1952

These make music
She's a founder

By L. ROBERT RIEBS
Special to Record-Eagle

"FOUNDER" — A title justly earned for founding or assisting in beginning something which has promise of being an asset to an organization or a community! It also implies being a part of a solid base upon which projects of unlimited value can grow and thrive. A synonym might indicate "one who begins" any type of activity. In some instances, there might be a group brought together to found or start a business, philanthropic movement or other civic activity. In any event, it is a mutual undertaking intended to benefit the group or area and promote its effectiveness.

Musician/teachers are often founders

Elnora Milliken
... 'one who begins'

Elnora tried everything she could to bring people to the symphony. To recruit audience members, Elnora held dinner parties at her home before evening concerts. This made for a busy evening: cooking the food, serving four couples, and then getting ready to play in the symphony. She always told people: "You're not too busy to come to our symphony."

Elnora, Louise and Carol formed a string trio and played chamber music in people's homes as a benefit. They also held a waltz evening at the Park Place hotel. Dr. Paz would dance waltzes with people from the audience while Elnora and her fellow string players provided the waltz music.

Supporting the symphony was a big job, and Elnora knew she needed help, so she organized a support group for the symphony, called the Women's Symphony Association. She had seen similar "friends" groups at other symphonies, and understood the critical role they played in on-going fundraising and stirring up interest. The Women's group held bridge parties and canasta parties to raise interest in the symphony, and held Silver Teas and fashion shows. Everyone pitched in to help sell geraniums – 1,500 potted plants – all for classical music.

From the beginning, Elnora and her friends wanted the symphony to be for children as well as adults. Besides free tickets for children, they visited local schools and brought instruments for the children to touch and try. Elnora and Mozelle Sawyer, another violinist, would play duets, and they showed children a short film called "Instruments of the Symphony."

The symphony, and forming the symphony, was part of the Milliken children's childhood. Often the children would be in the car while their mother went in to meetings to ask people for money, or they'd answer calls about the symphony at home. The children came to concerts and some rehearsals. Elnora even brought JP to rehearsal in his crib once when she couldn't find a sitter.

With the exception of oboes and trombones, the symphony was well balanced. At times the symphony posted an ad: "Help Wanted! Trombones." At another point, the symphony had all the orchestra instruments but had too many flutes. Other newspaper ads tried to entice new audience members and emphasized community:

"Music belongs to the people. This is your Community Symphony Orchestra."

"It's fine to wear ski clothes to the Sunday afternoon concert if it's a good day on the slopes."

"Enjoyment of Music is not limited to those who know music – for music speaks to the heart of everyone."

The idea of a community symphony and Elnora's passion for music caught on. Traverse City fell in love with its symphony orchestra. Soon locals were referring to the high school auditorium on Seventh Street as "Traverse City's Orchestra Hall." Some people were simply drawn by Elnora's magnetism. One violinist declared she wouldn't be in the symphony unless she got to sit next to Elnora Milliken, so Elnora obligingly moved back several stands to sit with her.

One spring, a March snowstorm threatened to shut down the concert. Many musicians got stuck in the blizzard, including Louise Williams, whose car was stuck. She abandoned the car and arrived by snowshoes, carrying her violin under one arm. Another memorable moment was when Elnora invited Les Biederman to come on stage and play a violin solo before the concert. Les gamely "played" the violin she handed him, but a musician behind the curtains actually played the music.

Pedro Paz conducted the Traverse symphony for six seasons. His last concert was May 1958, and all agreed that his high standards had elevated the symphony to a new level. The board brought in an interim conductor from Midland, Wilford Crawford, for one year, and then hired William Yarborough in 1959 to be the orchestra's first resident conductor.

William Yarborough was from the Purdue Symphony. "He was a character!" Elnora said. "He didn't press his coat or bother about his shoes. He was not here in the world all the time, he was an eccentric. But he was a good musician."

ELNORA LIKED PEOPLE TO BE COLORFUL
"LIKE SPRING FLOWERS"

ELNORA IS HONORED BY THE TRAVERSE SYMPHONY ORCHESTRA AND CONDUCTOR KEVIN RHODES IN 2011

The symphony changed its name to the Traverse Symphony Orchestra in 1985 and gradually began to transform from a volunteer orchestra to a full, professional, paid symphony. In the 1980s, musicians began getting paid and by 2001 the symphony had become professional. Elnora continued to play with the symphony through forty-three seasons. "Every concert was wonderful to me," she said. Today the Traverse Symphony presents eight to ten concerts per year, with a core group of sixty musicians under the direction of conductor Kevin Rhodes. They also offer a Saturday series of free music programs for children.

"It's really a first-class symphony now," said Elnora. "You don't have to go to Chicago or New York. Kevin Rhodes is so wonderful and the musicians are excellent."

OLD TOWN PLAYHOUSE

With the symphony up and running, Elnora remembered the thrill of acting in high school and the fun of Northwestern University's Wa-mu shows. "I loved acting. I got the idea: we have a symphony Why couldn't we have a playhouse?"

It was about a year after little Wendy had died. Elnora had been throwing herself into her music, and had begun taking lessons at Interlochen. It was at Interlochen that she met a new friend, Camilla Demoose who taught drama at Interlochen during the summers. She called her up.

"We need a playhouse," she said.

"Oh, Elnora, you don't know how much work a playhouse is!" Camilla responded. She had lived in Grand Rapids and knew about community theater, having worked at the Grand Rapids Civic Theatre.

Elnora was not dissuaded. She continued to call Camilla every week and talk about her idea for a community playhouse. "Nothing stops me," said Elnora. "If I'm determined to do something, if I have an idea, then I want to carry it through."

Finally Elnora wore her down. Camilla called one night: "Elnora, you and Father (Dr. John) come over and I'll go down in the basement and get the bylaws." John and Elnora went over to the Demoose house immediately. That was the beginning of the Traverse City Civic Players.

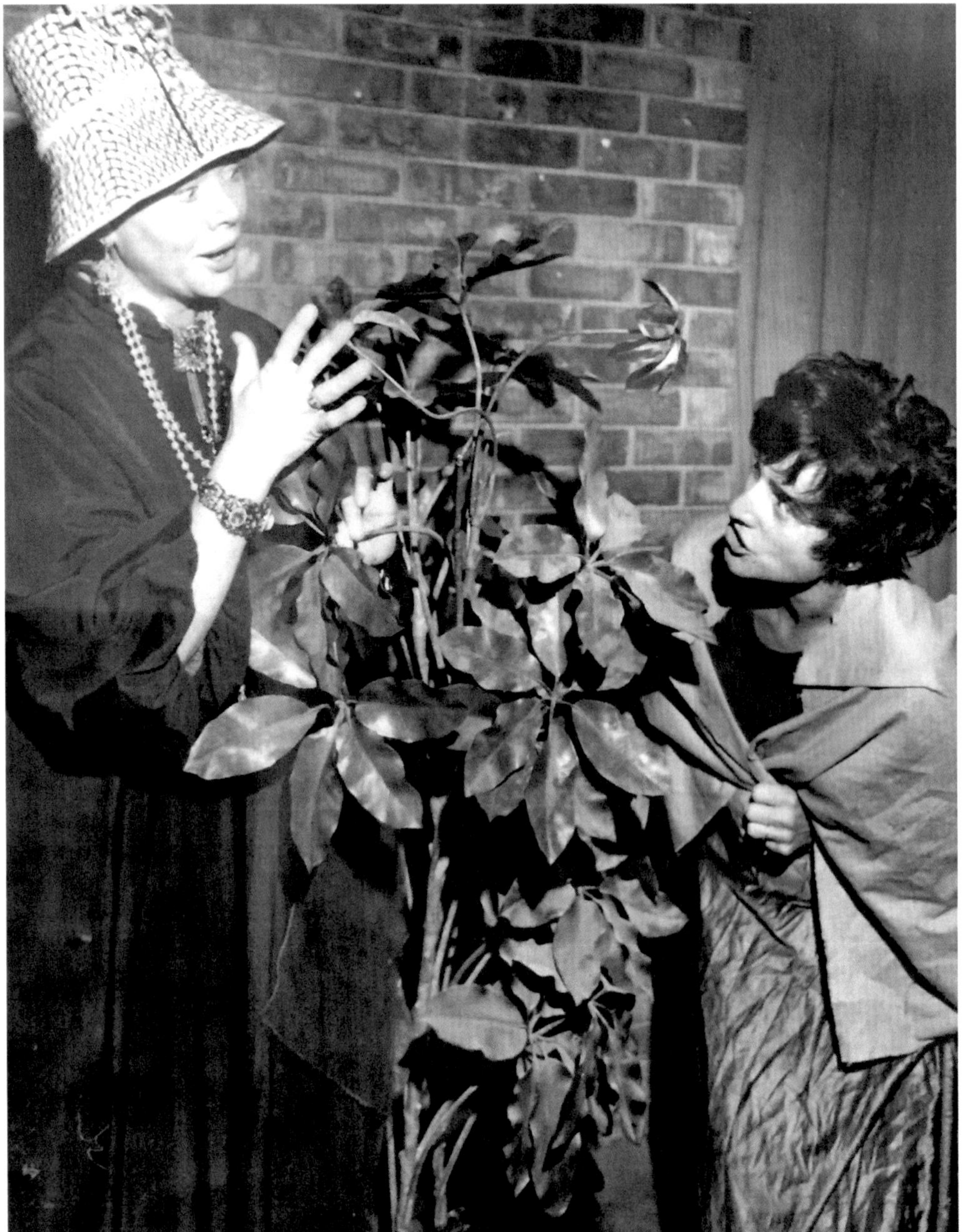

Camilla and Elnora gathered fellow theater enthusiasts to stage their first play, the comedy You Can't Take it With You, which opened in April 1960. They rehearsed at the school bus garage, and performed in the brand-new Traverse City high school, now called Traverse City Central. Elnora played the role of the leading lady, Alice Sycamore, and Camilla directed. Elnora's lover in the show was played by a local minister, Rev. Donn Doten, of Central Methodist church, which caused some amusement. "Father's here!" Camilla would call out when Dr. John arrived to watch the rehearsal. "Let's go through the love scene." Elnora blushed deeply whenever John watched the rehearsals, especially when Elnora had to say "I love you" three times and kiss Rev. Doten the third time.

On Opening Night, Elnora's family sent a surprise telegram to her dressing room: "Congratulations and best wishes! Love, John, Sherry, Jim and Penny." When Elnora saw the telegram delivery person, she was thrilled. "'Oh, I'm a star!' she thought. "I felt like a real actress."

The first play was a great success. It played to capacity audiences both nights. The Record-Eagle described the crowd and said the play's reception showed that an "all-amateur civic theater is wanted as a permanent institution in Traverse City." Elnora had instinctively known that. She also knew that the best way to gain support was by staging a play. "You can only keep inspiration in people if you do something, not just talk," she said.

Local theater had tried to get off the ground once before, in 1938. A group called the Traverse City Community Players met at the Park Place to do dramatic readings, but they never staged a play and by that time the daily newspaper was already full of stories about the Nazis. The outbreak of World War II derailed the group soon after.

After You Can't Take it With You, which launched with a budget of fifty dollars, the TC Civic Players got organized to create a business structure for the new theater group. The core group involved four couples: Elnora and John Milliken, Camilla and N.G. Damoose, Doug and Margaret Hill, and Bob and Barb Bradford. "Everybody likes to act," said Elnora "But nobody likes the details of paperwork. They didn't want to run a theater." Elnora asked John if he would help out on the business side as board president.

The first playhouse board formed in May 1960 with John as president, Camilla as vice president, and included many pioneering Traverse City names, such as Helen Osterlin. The Board met in medical buildings, at the Carnegie library on Sixth Street, and at the Chamber of Commerce. The Civic Players continued to stage shows at the high school for five years and then performed at the Park Place dome for seven years. The Park Place had more room than the high school, and was good for performances, but storing props, sets and costumes was more difficult, and rehearsals were held in a hodge-podge of locations. Rehearsals were held all over town: in the old airport buildings and church basements, or sometimes in a vacant bank building or warehouse. Once a rat chewed through a costume stored overnight at the airport.

The Civic Players presented their first full season of theater in 1960-61 with three comedies: The Silver Whistle (fall), Bell, Book and Candle (winter), and Arsenic and Old Lace in the spring. Season tickets sold for three dollars and a single performance was one dollar and a quarter. Dr. John had a role in The Silver Whistle, where he had three lines. During the performance he got his lines mixed up and said "goddamn whistle" too early, causing confusion among the other players.

When the Civic Players staged Arsenic and Old Lace that spring, April 1961, Elnora, Camilla and Dorothy Stulen, another enthusiastic actor, convinced their husbands and other city commissioners to make cameo appearances on stage at the end of the play. Dr. John and Frank Stulen both served on the city commission, and Camilla's husband was the city manager at the time. In the end, N.G. Damoose and the entire Traverse City commission appeared as dead bodies in Arsenic and Old Lace.

When JP was four years old, Elnora played the title character Agatha, in All Because of Agatha. Agatha was performed in 1966 at the Park Place hotel. As Agatha, a witch living in a haunted house, Elnora had to scream a lot. That wasn't hard. Elnora loved to scream. She'd even had a part in a play in second grade where she had to scream. The second grade play was performed in the school gym, and when young Elnora screamed and looked out at the audience, she thought: "Oh, isn't this fun? Everyone's frightened!" Now she was thrilled to be cast as Agatha and get a new chance to scream on stage. She practiced her screaming at home.

As Agatha, Elnora swept on stage in a dramatic entrance, screaming, with thunder and lightning and stage mist swirling about. Young JP was sitting in the audience watching the performance at the Park Place. When the screams stopped, JP's little voice cried out: "Is that my mama?" The audience started to laugh. To restore the mood, Elnora repeated her dramatic stage entrance and screamed again.

TRAVERSE CITY CIVIC PLAYERS

presents

"ALL BECAUSE OF AGATHA"

A Play in Three Acts

by Jonathan Troy

PARK PLACE MOTOR INN CONVENTION DOME

Dramatists Play Service, Inc.

Directed by MRS. RICHARD CRAMPTON

— THE CAST —
(in order of appearance)

Duff O'Hara	Chuck Preston
Joan O'Hara	Donna Lautner
Mrs. VanBuren	Nancy Preston
Mrs. Boggs	Laura Walton
Ethel	Dazey Kerr
Dr. Randolph	Ralph Hott
Thelma Breckenridge	Edith Anderson
Flip Cannon	Norm Dill
Madam LaSolda	Joanna Nesbit
Agatha Forbes	Elnora Milliken

Elnora brought her music to the playhouse, too. For Design for Murder, she played the part of Celia on stage, and also played her violin for the show, as part of a string quartet that recorded "Tonight we Love." Sometimes she played in the orchestra instead of acting. She loved playing her violin as part of the playhouse's very first musical, Guys and Dolls, in 1969.

Early plays cost around $675 to produce, including royalties, sets, costumes, publicity, director and auditorium fees. The group was stunned to learn that royalties to produce a big show like Guys and Dolls would cost $1,500. Like the symphony, the playhouse had to find a way to raise enough money. They soon gathered a loyal membership base of 300-400 people, and hosted dinners, magic shows, readings, one-act plays and a Men's Style Show. Elnora helped out co-chairing events and playing in musical variety shows. She also taught acting to children as part of an early children's theater effort in 1967.

The Civic Players was bursting with energy. It renamed itself the Old Town Playhouse, and relocated to its permanent home, the First Christian Church building on the corner of Eighth and Cass Streets in the early 1970s. Of course, it took extensive renovations to transform the church into a theater. The transformation included removing the stained glass windows and auctioning off pews. By 1975 the Playhouse made the big step and bought the building.

Elnora remained involved and attended shows, but didn't make time to act anymore. "I tried to do everything. I tried, but I also had the symphony, the Garden Club, my children, Dr. John, my husband, and my TV program."

The Old Town Playhouse never forgot its origins. It credits Elnora as the one main person responsible for starting the theater company, and calls her the "driving force." Over the next fifty-five years, the Playhouse continued to grow and thrive. They now offer a full season of plays and musicals, encourage new playwrights, have added a studio theater, and created a vibrant Young Company which involves hundreds of children and presents five shows a year in addition to year-round workshops and classes.

AT THE OLD TOWN
PLAYHOUSE'S JUNE 2013
BLACK & WHITE GALA
WEARING A CREATION
BY DEREK WOODRUFF

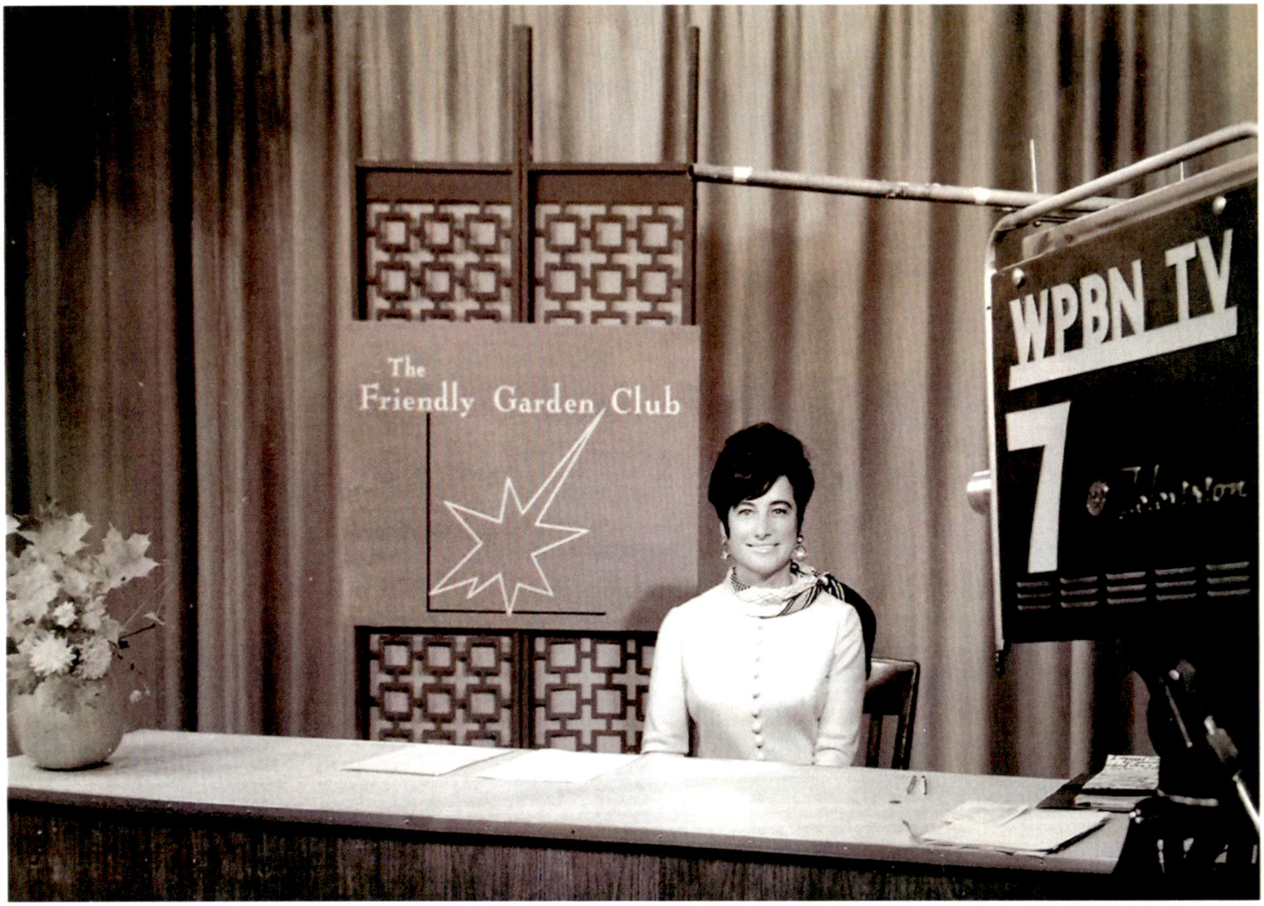
The
Friendly Garden Club
WPBN TV
7

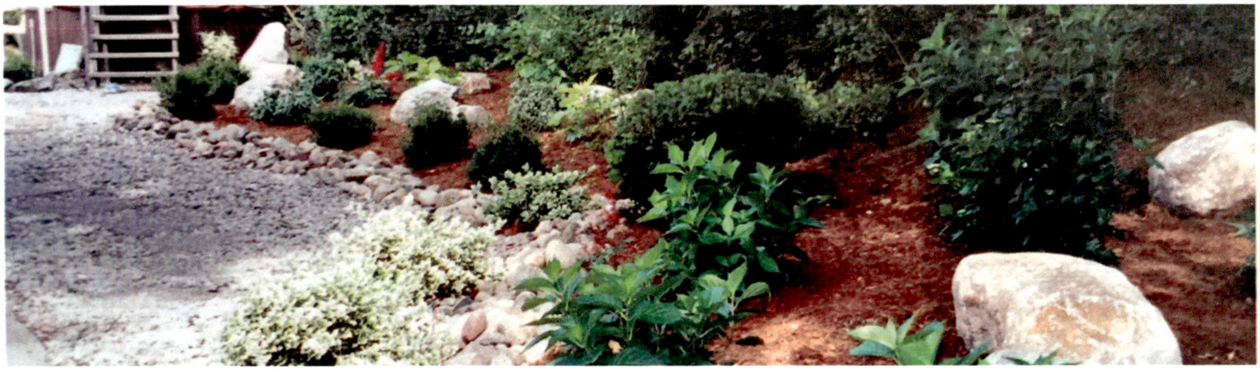

PART VI

MUSIC, GARDENS
AND *A*DVENTURES

THE FRIENDLY
GARDEN CLUB

Besides theater and music, Elnora followed her parents' love of gardening. She adored flowers and flower arranging, and soon became active in the Friendly Garden Club. When she first joined, club members asked her to be in charge of publicity. Elnora asked the club president if there was anything she could do for the Garden Club on the radio or TV. "I've done so much performing, it would come naturally," she said. Soon Elnora was meeting with Les Biederman who was in the radio business and owned TV channel 7/4. Les said: "I'll give you half an hour of TV programming time for free." Elnora had done a few radio ads in the past on behalf of the Milliken's department store, so she had some experience.

She called her TV program "The Friendly Garden Club of the Air." The show ran for sixteen years on WTON and WTCM, with Elnora as the host. Like Barbara Walters, she always liked to have a guest on each program. Elnora followed Barbara's style to begin each program, announcing: "Good afternoon and welcome to the Friendly Garden Club of the Air, a series of programs by the Friendly Garden Club. My name is Elnora Milliken, and my guest today is Joy of Cooking author, Irma Rombauer. She'll tell you some gardening tips for this time of year." Elnora's program won state and national awards and attracted listeners as far as the Upper Peninsula, which was unusual at the time.

Elnora also presented gardening tips on TV channel 7/4. During Cherry Festival one year, Elnora shared cherries jubilee. The jubilee recipe included liqueur, and when she lit the candle underneath the cherries jubilee caught on fire — live on TV. Everyone liked the disaster so much the TV station did a replay of the Cherries Jubilee on Fire.

Another time Elnora was called to be a TV guest at the last minute when the scheduled guest was caught in a February snowstorm. Elnora brought a branch of forsythia she'd been forcing to bloom in the shower at home. The TV host excitedly cried: "Look what Elnora found in her garden!" It was obvious the host didn't know much about gardening, but Elnora didn't want to lie or embarrass him on live TV. She quickly changed the subject, saying: "I'm so glad to be here on your show today."

One of Elnora's great loves was ikebana, the art of Japanese flower arranging. Ikebana emphasizes asymmetrical form and empty space in the arrangement, using a minimal number of flowers or branches to create a sense of harmony between humans and nature. Ikebana looks simple but it can take years to master. Elnora's creative spirit thrived with the ikebana art form, and her arrangements won several regional and national ikebana awards.

With all her activities, Elnora rushed about the house often in a half-dressed state going from one rehearsal to another meeting. "I was always going somewhere," she said. "The children got used to seeing me like that. People said I was vivacious. If your personality is fast, it's hard to go slowly."

Elnora's TV program was so popular that the TV station staff began bringing all the recording equipment to her home. She recorded the last programs from her house on Peninsula Drive.

ONE OF ELNORA'S MANY AWARD-WINNING
JAPANESE FLOWER ARRANGEMENTS

MUSIC AND INTERLOCHEN
PUBLIC RADIO

All this time Elnora was pursuing her own musical study. She and Louise Williams both studied piano with Dorothy Curtis, an excellent pianist who lived in Minneapolis. Dorothy taught piano in Traverse City seasonally when she summered at Neahtawanta, on Old Mission Peninsula. Elnora auditioned to be accepted as one of Dorothy's students. While she was waiting for the results, she joined a group of women to play nine-hole golf. The day was hot and the women were arguing. Elnora sighed and promised herself: "If I get in to study with Dorothy, I'm going to quit this nine-hole golf!" She did. Soon Elnora was studying piano with Dorothy, and summers became a lovely time for family, piano, tennis and boating.

Music followed Elnora wherever she went, including on out-of-town business trips with Dr. John to medical conferences. During one trip near Lansing, John said to Elnora: "Why don't you get up and play some of those jazz songs? They'd loan you a violin." So Elnora did. She loved creating music wherever she was. She continued to play string trios with Louise Williams and Carol Kempton, once performing for the grand opening of the megastore Meijer. The trio members were paid fifty dollars each. Elnora saved her fifty dollars to remember the event.

Besides creating her own TV program, Elnora was one of the founders of a classical music station, 88.7, at Interlochen. The arts center had dreamed of having its own public radio station for some time, and in 1963 Elnora traveled to Chicago with Thom Paulsen and Helen Osterlin to explore the possibility of starting a brand new classical music radio station. During their two-day trip to Chicago, Elnora, Thom and Helen learned they were on the right path for success. One major step was to get permission from the Association of Public Broadcasting.

Elnora served on the Board of Interlochen Public Radio for twenty years and was thrilled to have a classical music radio station for the Traverse City area. "I always like to introduce people who are interested to what I'm interested in," she said.

MILLIKEN MEDICAL ORCHESTRA

Not content to found one orchestra, Elnora founded two. The second orchestra was composed of doctors in the Milliken Medical Building. "I got ambitious," said Elnora. "I found out most of the doctors used to play an instrument in high school." She formed them into the "Milliken Medical Orchestra" and told them: "If you find instruments and promise to come rehearsals, I'll buy the music," which she did.

The Milliken Medical Orchestra began with two violins, one guitar, two clarinets, a trumpet and a baritone, with Elnora on violin and piano. Dr. John played the other violin. She led them through popular songs such as "When the Saints Come Marching In," "La Cucaracha" and Christmas carols. One year they played Mexican Christmas songs wearing sombreros. The doctor-musicians presented Elnora with a bouquet of flowers every year and with a trophy one year to show their appreciation. Elnora cherishes the trophy. Each year she looks at it and admires the flowers, so appreciative of the musical group of doctors who make up the

ELNORA AND JOHN READY FOR A TSO EVENT

MILLIKEN MEDICAL MUSIC REHEARSAL
FOR THE ANNUAL OFFICE CHRISTMAS
PARTY

DR. JOHN MILLIKEN AND DR. BILL HOWARD

orchestra. Fifty years later the Milliken Medical Orchestra is still playing together and sharing the joy of music at Christmas time.

The group performs a Christmas concert once a year, and rehearses about four times before the concert. Elnora leads rehearsals from her family's Guest House #1. They meet early – at 7am – so busy doctors can go on to a full day of work. At times, when the group needs more practice, they rehearse downstairs in the lunchroom at the Milliken Medical Building. "The doctors often arrive at rehearsals with tired faces," said Elnora. "But leave smiling and so happy.

BOAT STORAGE IN THE FILED AT THE HOUSE ON PENINSULA DRIVE

BOATING AND RV TRIPS

As soon as Elnora and John arrived in Traverse City, they bought boats. Sailboats, and motor boats. Small boats and large boats. Being out on the water was one of their greatest joys.

One boat they named the Queen Mary. John was always changing the names of his boats, so after a while they decided to stop painting the names on the stern. Most of the boats they owned over the years were small enough to dock in front of the house. The largest one, a 32-foot motor boat, they kept at Darrow's harbor, now Harbor West.

John organized sunfish races and taught all the children to sail. Once Elnora spied a sailboat for sale at Murray's Boat Shop. "You like sailing so much," she told John. "It has a cabin and everything." John bought the boat, and Penny sailed it regularly by herself in high school. John loved giving the children the freedom to explore.

In town, they used the boats for social events. The Park Place used to show movies at night, and Elnora and John would arrive downtown by boat and invite friends to where the boat was docked. Elnora usually cooked a big pot of spaghetti chili, and afterwards they'd go to the movie or theater.

John's favorite places for boating besides the Grand Traverse Bay, were Beaver Island, Les Cheneaux Islands and the North Channel near Georgian Bay. Sometimes he also crossed Lake Michigan to Wisconsin. Elnora was thrilled the first time she saw the North Channel and its wild, rugged beauty. On trips to the North Channel they slept on the boat (the big boat had at least six bunks), but on trips to Beaver Island they stayed on shore in a vacation house they bought with several friends.

(OPPOSITE) BOAT STORAGE AT THE FAMILY RESIDENCE

Life on Beaver Island was calm and quiet. The family often cooked outdoors and enjoyed the views and breeze. But the boat crossing to reach Beaver Island or the mainland could be rough. One time, John and Elnora watched anxiously for Sherry and Jim's boat to arrive back in Traverse City during a rough day with high waves. Another time the family was coming back from Beaver Island on the 32-foot boat. The water was so rough Elnora grew increasingly nervous and began to cry. Young JP, who was six-years-old at the time, said: "How do you think I feel, Mama? I can't even swim."

The roughest Beaver Island crossing took place when JP was fourteen. John, Elnora and JP, plus their guests, four other doctors and their wives, were trying to return to Charlevoix, the mainland port. The waves were about eighteen feet high that day. The lake was so rough that Elnora and the other wives decided to buy a ferry ticket and return to Charlevoix on the Beaver Island ferry. Even the ferry ride was difficult. "Everybody was throwing up," said Elnora. "I said to the captain: 'See that boat way out there? That's the boat all the doctors are on. Please make sure the bow comes up.'"

Meanwhile John, JP and the doctors were enduring a grueling six-hour crossing. The trip to Charlevoix usually took an hour. John trusted JP to help run the boat. The boat's canvas top broke, but they made it safely, the only small craft to dare the crossing that day. When Elnora met the boat in Charlevoix at last, she asked JP: "How was it?" He bluntly said: "Mom, it was bad. Very bad."

Sometimes misadventures also took place on land. The first time the family explored the North Channel they ate lunch at a little café up on a hill in Ontario. Afterwards, everyone got sick and threw up. That episode didn't diminish their love for the North Channel. Besides, they always had a doctor with them for adventures like this.

Elnora knew how to run the boats, but John was the big sailor. She trusted him to keep the boat upright. One day John invited Elnora for a short sail on West Bay to Bryant Park in Traverse City on the sunfish. "Sure," she said. She always felt safe with John on board. The wind came up as they sailed south. "John, will we flip over?" Elnora asked. "No, not in the world," John answered. "No way this boat could tip over." The next thing they knew the boat flipped. Elnora screamed and screamed. Then she discovered she could stand up on the sandy bottom. John and Elnora were in shallow water close to Bryant Park, and had an audience on the beach looking at the mishap.

ELNORA AND PENNY WITH
FRED AND EVE ISON

(BOTTOM)
DOCTOR JOHN'S
BOATS AS SEEN
FROM THE FRONT
TERRACE OF
THE HOUSE ON
PENINSULA DRIVE

Boats were for swimming, too. John would stop the boat en route to Beaver Island and encourage the children to jump off and swim. They wore life jackets and had a life ring on a rope in the water that they could easily reach. The family also sailed on the bay frequently and went swimming there. When the children were grown, John and Elnora often invited couples to join them boating. These trips were always fun, and sometimes memorable – for instance when a guest had to go to the bathroom which was located under the bow. "We could see him smiling back at us from the bow, but he couldn't get out. He was stuck," said Elnora. The memory still makes her giggle years later. "Something always happens on boat trips," said Elnora. "But with boating you always go back if you had a good time."

A particularly eventful boat trip happened in the late 1970s when John and Elnora were hosting their Japanese friend Teruko Komesu, whose father owned a medical clinic in Japan. They headed to one of John's favorite places, Goose Island, one of the islands in Les Cheneaux, east of the Mackinac Bridge. John spied another boat less than a mile off his starboard side and powered up his boat to race him. The islands there were not well charted. John knew Goose Island, which was uninhabited, and also knew there was an extensive shoal right off the island, but that day he got mixed up and raced his boat directly into the Goose Island reef, smashing the boat on the rocks at forty miles per hour. Teruko and Elnora were both screaming. Elnora thought they were sinking.

John knew he needed help fast. He radioed the Coast Guard, based in St. Ignace. "This is dumb-head Milliken," he said. "I've just careened into Goose Island reef and I think I need help." The Coast Guard sent a "mother ship" to rescue them, a boat about 38 ft. long. They sent a raft to the reef to rescue John and his two frightened passengers, Elnora and Teruko, and soon everybody was aboard the mother ship. The women retreated to a corner and wouldn't speak to John. When the Coast Guard boat arrived on the mainland in Cedarville, a crowd of about thirty people came running to meet them. "Where's dumb-head Milliken?" they wanted to know.

That evening John hired a towboat to rescue their boat left on the reef. The operation required skin-divers to help free it. The boat was battered and the two outdrive motors were badly damaged, but the hull was still intact. "I've been through many dangerous things with John, but we've always come out all right," said Elnora. Elnora asked to keep the boat's two damaged propellers, and now the propellers greet visitors at the entrance to the Milliken home.

Family travels were not all by boat. The family went on ski vacations and visited New York City, and John and Elnora traveled together often for medical conferences. John bought a 30-plus-foot Air Stream for family camping trips. The first time they used the Air Stream they camped in Florida with all the children. Elnora liked the campground but found she couldn't get any peace with four children in the bus, so she took to reading her book in the bathroom and hiding there for privacy.

Years later, John and Elnora bought a motor home, and traveled with Penny and JP to Florida for a medical meeting. JP would serve his mother breakfast on the bus while John drove. In Florida, John left Elnora, Penny and JP with the motor home in the campground, and John set off to hitchhike to the conference. He got a ride right away from a kind-hearted woman. She said to John: "My husband said I should never do this, but you looked so nice."

Back in Traverse City, the motor home had local adventures, too. On his day off, John liked to invite friends for Sunday breakfast. "We'll serve you breakfast on the bus!" he cried. They drove by their guests' houses to pick them up, and served a cooked breakfast, often with cocktails, parking the motor home on a beautiful spot by the beach.

Other times they invited friends for parties that might include impromptu swimming. "We went skinny dipping in the bay," Elnora said. "One time a guest slipped and got poison ivy! We had all kinds of happenings."

Once Elnora and John were driving to Minnesota to attend the wedding of Muffi's son when John ran out of gas. They were stranded in the Upper Peninsula. Elnora stood by the highway with her violin case and tried to get a ride while John walked to town to get gas. By the time someone stopped to help Elnora, John was back with the gas can.

Summer trips often included alumni reunions at Amherst College. John loved Amherst and his fraternity, and they visited at least every five years. Sometimes they arrived via motor home with all the children. One year Elnora and John played a prank on their Amherst friends. They'd recently bought wigs for fun – Elnora had a blond wig, and John's was dark. "Why don't we bring our wigs to Amherst and put them on?" Elnora suggested with a mischievous twinkle in her eye. During an Amherst reunion dance, John left the room and put on his wig. When he returned, he asked Elnora to dance, astounding his fraternity brothers. They said to each other: "That person is certainly getting fresh with Elnora!"

A deeply memorable trip took place years later when Elnora and John visited Italy. They traveled to the very village where Elnora's mother, Lucia, had once lived. They saw her mother's grade school and the family orchard land, and stayed with a cousin who was a druggist. Lucia herself had gone back to Italy only once to see her father's grave. Elnora visited Italy again in 2011 when Penny arranged a special family trip. This was a three generations trip that included Elnora, Penny, Penny's daughter, Jennifer, and Sherry's daughter, Halle. Penny contacted extended cousins ahead of time so they were warmly welcomed by family in France and Italy.

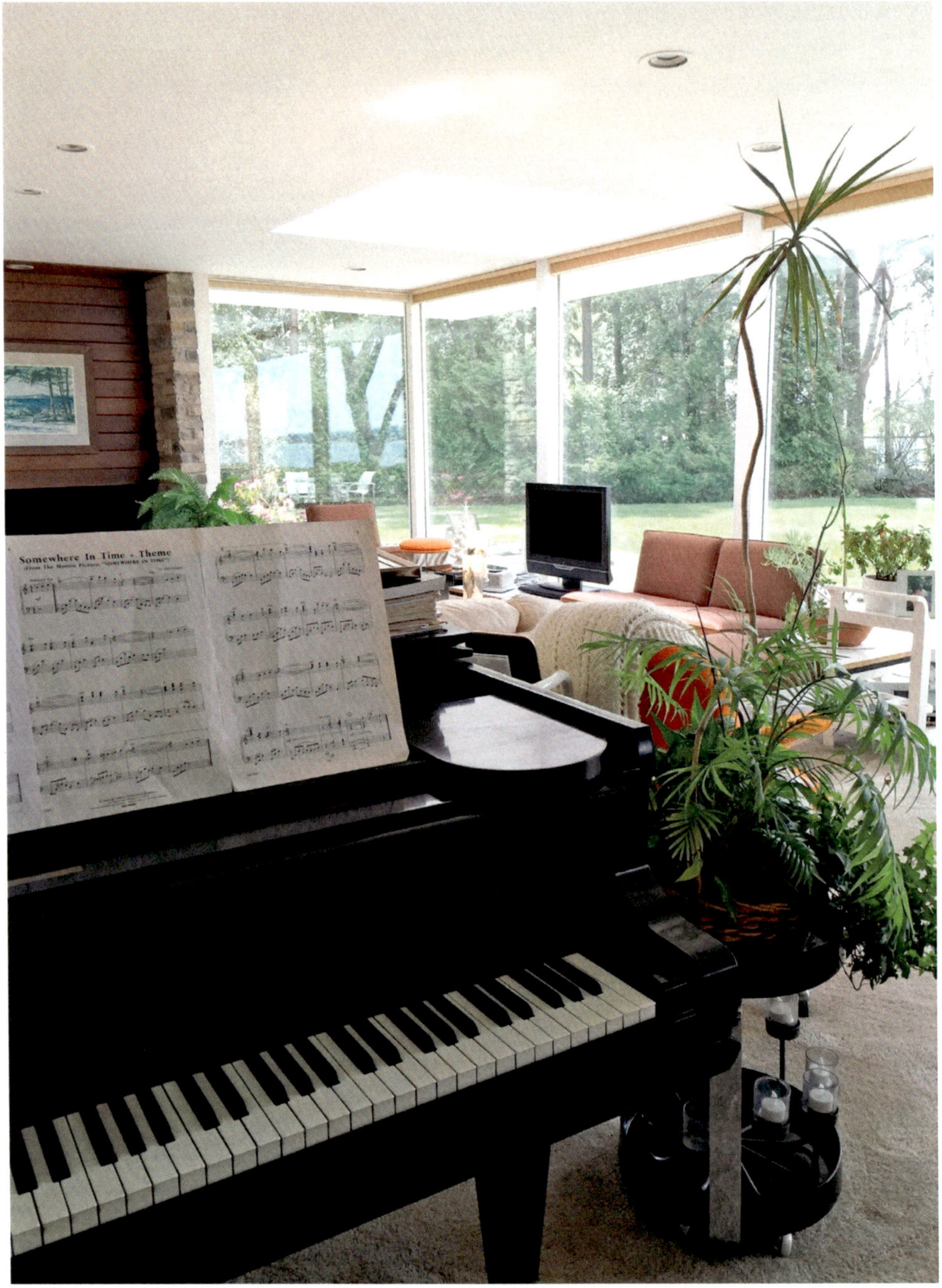
Somewhere In Time - Theme

PART VII

Advancing

Every afternoon Elnora sits down at the piano to play. She slides onto the black bench before Wendy's grand piano in the living room, and plays Debussy's "Claire de Lune" or another favorite. She still has the Czerny piano technique book she used in fourth grade. The corners and edges are torn with a lifetime of use. "I know them so well," she says. "I don't play as beautifully as I once did. Now I play to relax and enjoy."

MUSICAL CHAIRS AT THE 'END OF THE SUMMER' FAMILY GATHERING

GROWING FAMILY

The children are grown now and Elnora has nine grandchildren. She still has her mother's blue glass vase with the scalloped top, and fills it with peonies and roses, especially on Mother's Day. "It makes me always think of their garden. They spent all their life in the garden." Her beloved John died in 2008 after sixty-four years of marriage. Elnora's memories of their first dates and dances are as vivid as ever.

Sherry married Bob Reum and they live in Chicago, with a house in Wayne, IL and a condo downtown. Sherry graduated from the University of Michigan and received an MBA from Columbia University. Bob is CEO of Amsted Industries, an industrial conglomerate. They have three children: Courtney, Carter and Halle. The two brothers first worked for Goldman Sachs and then struck out on their own as entrepreneurs. The duo garnered attention from the Today Show and from Goldman Sachs, which selected them as being among the country's "100 Most Intriguing Entrepreneurs" in 2014. Their sister, Halle, makes her career in fashion as a style consultant in Hollywood.

Jim is a doctor of internal medicine and lives locally in Traverse City. His office is in the Milliken Medical Building, and he specializes in internal medicine, critical care, pulmonary care and sleep. Jim married Mary Beth Ratty and they have two children, Jay and Christine. Mary Beth manages the Milliken Medical Building, and takes care of everything, including Elnora's roses. Their son, Jay, is developing into an excellent public speaker and lives in Los Angeles where he is an entrepreneur. Their daughter Christine graduated from Michigan State University where she played tennis on the university team. She is studying to be a physician's assistant at Grand Valley State University and graduates in December 2015.

Penny was a marketing executive for The Walt Disney Company for many years, both in Paris and Los Angeles. She recently moved to Seattle to become CEO of Her Interactive, a company that develops Nancy Drew video games. She has one daughter, Jennifer, who graduated from the University of California-Berkeley and is State Director for Environment Florida.

John G. Milliken, M.D., F.A.C.P.
John O. Zachman, M.D.
William A. Howard, M.D.
S. Lee Warnaar, M.D.
Richard D. Entz, M.D.
Walter K. Meeker, M.D.
David J. Straight, M.D.
B. MacDougall
INTERNAL MEDICINE

JP is also a doctor, a gastroenterologist and has his practice in the Milliken Medical Building. He married Darcy Doebler, and they have three children: Jack, Maggie and Kelly. The children all love boating and tennis, playing frequently at their grandparents' tennis court on Peninsula Drive. Jack majored in business at Michigan State University and and after working at a digital marketing agency, is now getting his MBA at MSU. Maggie is also in business. She graduated from Miami University in Ohio and works in Chicago. Kelly, the youngest of the grandchildren, is a junior at Michigan State University.

Elnora's father and mother are buried in Minneapolis in a military cemetery, since her father served briefly in World War I. Elnora thinks of them often and continues many of their joys and seasonal routines. For example, every January, Elnora still cuts forsythia branches and brings them indoors, keeping the branches in the shower for a week to promote the buds. Her children would not be surprised. Over the years, they grew used to sharing the shower with branches of cherries and forsythia. "There goes Mother again with her branches!" they said. "We have to take showers again with her forsythia!"

(OPPOSITE) LEFT TO RIGHT: DR. JIM MILLIKEN,
DR. JOHN MILLIKEN, DR. JP MILLIKEN
(THIS PAGE, BOTTOM) FAMILY CHRISTMAS
GATHERING, 2009

SUNDAY, AUGUST 8, 2010 — WWW.GRANDTRAVERSEINSIDER.COM — PAGE 3A

INSIDER TRAVERSE

TRAVERSE CITY

Creative Expression

Japanese art of Ikebana unites local floral enthusiasts

By KATIE BEDARD
Contributing Writer

With most people living life at a hectic pace, many wonder if there is ever a chance to slow down and reflect on some of the simpler pleasures often overlooked.

Ikebana, the Japanese art of flower arranging known to facilitate tranquility, relaxation and a communion with nature, is an inspirational pastime.

"Ikebana is making flowers come alive," said Elnora Milliken, a founding member of the local Ikebana International Mizuwmi Chapter #165. "Ikebana strengthens our connection with nature and self expression, gives us joy, satisfaction and culture."

The name itself inspires such spiritual goals.

"'Ike' (represents) three verbs in the Japanese language," Milliken said, "to place, to live and to make life clear. 'Bana' means flower or plant."

Ikebana is the art of using flowers and plant material both in a paint and a sculptural form, Milliken also said. Some arrange flowers, while others paint flowers, leaves, branches and other plant matter.

Ikebana is also a modern, more minimalistic art form that allows anyone to experiment in self-expression.

"(It) gives everyone the chance to be creative," Milliken said. "Additionally, flowers beautifully arranged in a vase comfort people in our daily lives. Flowers make you happy."

The local Mizuwmi chapter began in the early 1970s when a Japanese friend of Milliken's began teaching her friends and acquaintances about the art form, and the subject became so popular they decided to start their own chapter.

Chapter #165 is affiliated with the international organization, Ikebana International, which means that a member is welcome at all other affiliates, Milliken said.

Friendship though flowers

"The theme of Ikebana International is 'friendship through flowers.' Those belonging to the club here could go (anywhere) to an exhibition or chapter and they will be welcome."

"We are a very active chapter," Milliken said. "We meet every month, on the first Wednesday."

The group, which numbers about 20, focuses on learning about different forms and schools of arranging, with classes, discussions and demonstrations at every meeting.

On Aug. 12, the group will also be presenting their biennial luncheon at the Elks' Club.

"It's a very beautiful event," Milliken said.

If you go

There is limited seating for the Aug. 12 luncheon, which begins at noon and ends at 3 p.m. Tickets are $12 per person. For details or to reserve tickets, call 231-947-1946 or 231-947-5496.

Photo by Katie Bedard
Elnora Milliken displays one of her Ikebana pieces. Ikebana, the Japanese art of flower arranging, is known to facilitate tranquility, relaxation and a communion with nature

The meeting will include a light buffet lunch, flower arranging demonstrations, seminars, exhibition tables and Japanese items such as books, kenzans, containers and much more for sale.

The event will be informational and inspirational for beginners, visitors and seasoned members alike.

"(The art form of Ikebana) is timeless," Milliken said. "There is something of the artist in each of us."

ELNORA IN 2008 ON ISLAND VIEW ROAD

ALWAYS ADVANCING

"Vitality sweeps over me and I forget my age," says Elnora. Besides, in her counting system, she's not old at all. "I was born on Thanksgiving Day, November 25th, so I only age every eight years because that's how often Thanksgiving comes on November 25th," she says. "Never think of your age," she advises. "Advancing is a much better word. Do what you can to keep up your interests and always find something new and different. You'll feel better then as you advance."

Wherever you go in Traverse City, Elnora's spirit is captured in the vibrant arts organizations she helped found: the Traverse Symphony Orchestra, Old Town Playhouse, Interlochen Public Radio, and also the Milliken Medical Orchestra. When Interlochen director Jeffrey Kimpton interviewed her for a recent Interlochen Radio Program, "Island Cabin Discs," Elnora shared music good for dancing by Glenn Miller and George Gershwin. "I love to dance!" she said. "Either I cry, I smile or I dance. Music moves me." She also chose the Méditation from Thaïs, the piece she played as a solo for high school graduation. Whenever she's not playing the piano, her radio is tuned to 88.7, Interlochen Public Radio.

In 2012, the Traverse City Area Chamber of Commerce recognized Elnora with their "Distinguished Service Award," citing her notable accomplishments of launching the Traverse Symphony Orchestra and Old Town Playhouse. Chamber Board president Tony Anderson presented the award at the Grand Traverse Resort and Spa, and said: "She is a pioneer in spirit and an artist at heart." Many friends and family members attended the event, and the crowd of more than 800 people gave her a well-earned standing ovation.

REGION/STATE

NEWS FROM NORTHWEST LOWER MICHIGAN

Saturday, January 28, 2012

LOCAL NEWS EDITOR (231) 933-1472

"She is a pioneer in spirit and an artist at heart."

Tony Anderson, board chairman of the Traverse City Area Chamber of Commerce

Elnora Milliken, center, recipient of the Traverse City Area Chamber of Commerce's 2011 Distinguished Service Award, receives a standing ovation from a crowd that included U.S. Sen. Debbie Stabenow, D-Mich., left, on Friday evening at the Grand Traverse Resort & Spa in Acme. Milliken's daughter, Penny Milliken, right, is at her mother's side.

Record-Eagle/Jan-Michael Stump

CHAMBER SAYS BRAVO!

Elnora Milliken receives Distinguished Service Award

Elnora continued to play violin in the Traverse Symphony Orchestra until the 1993-94 season. Even then she came back as a guest player for one concert in 1998. Sherry and Bob created an endowment fund for the orchestra in her honor and the symphony has named the concertmaster/mistress chair the "Elnora Toldo Milliken Founder's Chair." Elnora hardly ever misses a concert. She has season tickets, and although she doesn't drive anymore, her friends, the Knodes, take her to the concerts. She still talks passionately about the symphony and tells people: "You're not too busy to go to the symphony concerts. You can take time for beautiful music."

Elnora also is a season subscriber to plays at the Old Town Playhouse, and loves its energy. She remains active with her beloved Friendly Garden Club, and regularly attends Ikebana meetings with friends. She enjoys Pilates and is also a regular participant of the local Economics Club, which meets at the Country Club.

The Milliken Medical Orchestra gathers each December for their traditional Christmas party and concert. At their most recent concert, Elnora played keyboard, her son Dr. Jim was one of the two clarinets, and her son Dr. JP played the baritone. Other medical musicians in the group included a saxophone, guitar, viola, flute, trumpet and bell ringers. They played "Jingle Bells," "Silver Bells," and other Christmas songs, with Dr. Entz playing the trumpet beautifully on "White Christmas."

ELNORA IN PARIS WITH JENNIFER AND PENNY (2011)

Today Elnora has three violins: her childhood violin from junior high that her mother and father bought for her, a violin one of Dr. John's patients gave him, and, of course, Wendy's violin from Interlochen. "My childhood violin has such a beautiful tone," says Elnora. "I know all my violins by tone. They're like my children." The violins are nearby in the "Music Room" at her home, and it comforts her to know that her three violins will go on making beautiful music. "They'll be making music into the future," she says. The thought makes her happy, for sharing joyous music is what Elnora's life has been all about.

For now, Elnora looks out from her kitchen table at the blue shining waters of West Grand Traverse Bay. She reads aloud a favorite saying, a blessing for her children and grandchildren: "May your day be filled with music, may your life be filled with song." Memories of music, love and laughter swirl around her. She remembers the night long ago she slept in a tree bathed in moonlight. "At midnight, there's not a sound," she says. "The moon is smiling. All alone in the moonlight now, I smile at the memories and happiness because they will live forever."

Elnora's memories are full of music and family. If you're quiet, perhaps you can hear snatches of the traditional Italian song "Santa Lucia," as Elnora's mother, Lucia, sings and her father, Pietro, plays the mandolin.

Sul mare luccica

L'astro d'argento

Placida è l'onda

Prospero il vento;

Venite all'agile

Barchetta mia;

Santa Lucia! Santa Lucia!

THANKSGIVING 1997, WAYNE, IL

MILLIKEN MEDICAL BUILDING

WHEN DR. JOHN PURCHASED THE LAND, HE KEPT THE LARGE ROCK AT THE CORNER OF THE TWO SIDEWALKS. NATIVE MICHIGAN INDIANS HAD PLACED IT ON THE LAND AND SAID REMOVING IT WAS BAD LUCK.

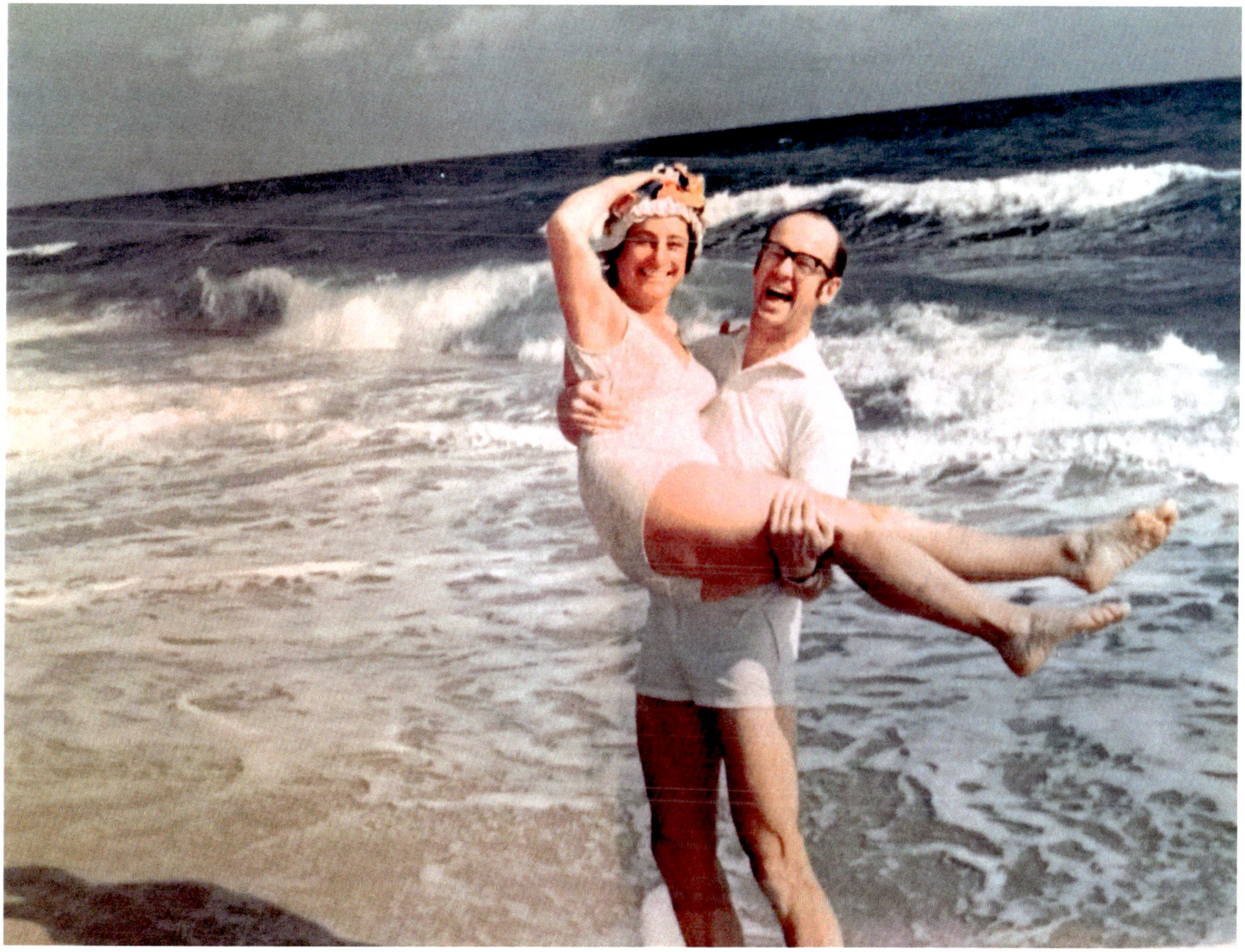

Made in the USA
Lexington, KY
15 April 2019